What Do You Know?

Editor: Claire Richardson
Design: Ann Salisbury
Production: Garry Lewis

What Do You Know?

Fascinating answers to questions on
everything from Astronomy to Zoology

Edited by Robert Matthews & Nick Smith

CARLTON
BOOKS

Acknowledgements

It is virtually impossible to have worked on *Focus* magazine as a journalist and not had some involvement in the questions and answers in this book – equally it impossible to name every single journalist ever to take up the quill in the name of the magazine. The following list therefore namechecks the principal researchers and contributors to the magazine over the past few years.

So thank you to: Ali MacArthur, Anna Fox, Antony Topazio, Debbie Butler, Caroline Green, Caroline Elliott, Caterina Gianota, Chris Edwards, Dickon Ross, Emma Bayley, Emma Young, Gaia Vince, Geoff Johnson (art direction), Gill Mullins, Hannah Khalil, Jess McAree, John Liddle, Keith Wilson, Ken Grimes (proofing), Kevin Hilton, Maggie Allen, Mike Papadimitrou, Paul Parsons, Paul Simpson, Pete Chan, Piers Bizony, Ruth Killick, Sarah Barnett, Sharon Ann Holgate, Simon Braund, Simon Reeve, Shaun Campbell, Shinji Toyoshima, Sophia Collins, Stéphane Breysse (picture editing), Susan Aldridge, Su-Yen Northill, Vicky Paterson, Zoe Willows.

Finally Robert and Nick wish to thank Emma Dally of the National Magazine Company, Claire Richardson of Carlton Books and our Assistant Editor Sally Palmer whose organisational and journalistic skills made the task of editing this book much easier than it should have been.

contents

Introduction

It's amazing how much we take for granted until we look around us. We're surrounded by questions: Why do clocks go clockwise? Why is the sky blue? Why do some people have curly hair? Why are there so few insects in the sea? Why is the number 13 so unlucky? Why is vitamin C good for you?

Humans are inquisitive by nature, but it is a lot easier to ask questions than it is to answer them. Perhaps it's for that very reason that question and answer format books are so popular. However, the book you have before you differs from the norm in three fundamental ways.

Firstly, *Questions and Answers* has grown out of the Q & A section of the monthly magazine *Focus* – a magazine that takes as its five editorial pillars: science, technology, nature, culture and adventure. And these necessarily form the orbit in which our questioners question – in other words, rather than random questions pitched in from out of the blue they fall within specific categories.

Secondly, although all the questions are from readers of *Focus* magazine, the answers are not. Unlike other Q & A books which rely on reader responses (which often contradict one another), our answers have all been researched by journalists qualified to comment, and in most instances they have secured quotes from the people most likely to know the answer (for example, the question "Is it true that Tenzing Norgay was the first man to reach the top of Mount Everest?" was largely answered by Sir Edmund Hillary himself).

Lastly, and perhaps most importantly, although the body of this book is written in a breezy journalistic style the content is of genuine information value – we've dispensed with frivolous questions and stuck to the truly intriguing ones.

It was the great twentieth-century poet W. H. Auden who once observed that, "to ask the hard question is simple". Had he been of a mind to elaborate he may well have added that to answer any question, hard or otherwise, requires more energy and resources than we can normally allocate in our daily lives. We're so preoccupied with questions like "where are the car keys?" or "where does the No. 45 bus go to?" that we forget to ask ourselves why it is that we don't drink pig's milk, or whether there's a mathematical explanation for why we all own so many odd socks, or indeed why the Moon is sometimes red…

Nick Smith

Nick Smith

Don't forget, if you have a burning question that you'd like to see answered in the next volume of *Questions and Answers* please email me at nick.smith@natmags.co.uk, or you can visit the *Focus* website at www.focusmag.co.uk

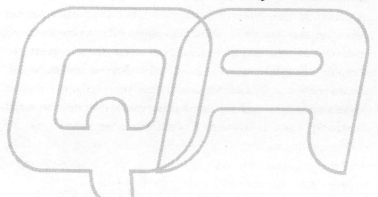

Astronauts,

Astronauts,

Telescopes

Telescopes

and the

and the

universe

universe

ⓐ How can you make telescopes more powerful?

ⓐ The short answer is make them bigger – but be careful how you do it. During the 1960s, the Soviet Union tried to prove its scientific superiority over the West by building a telescope at Mt Semirodriki in the Caucasus Mountains. The telescope's mirror was 6 metres in diameter – almost a metre wider than the world-famous Mt Palomar telescope in California. The attempt proved disastrous: the mirror was so big that it took days to come into thermal equilibrium with its surroundings, and was so plagued by wobbles and turbulence that it never really worked.

Ever since, the biggest telescopes have used very thin mirrors or lots of small mirrors under computer control. For example, the world's largest telescopes – the twin Keck telescopes on Mauna Kea, Hawaii – both have 10-metre mirrors made up of 36 hexagonal 1.8-metre mirrors.

Since the late 1980s, however, astronomers have been experimenting with a new way of building even more powerful telescopes. One method, known as interferometry, involves using two or more mirrors placed well apart from each other, and combining their individual images by computer.

Plans are underway to link the twin giant Keck telescopes in this way, to create a "virtual" telescope with a mirror effectively 85 metres in diameter – increasing to a staggering 100 metres when "outrigger" mirrors are arranged around the site. That will allow astronomers to make out detail on objects in space as fine as 0.005 arc-seconds – equivalent to being able to read a newspaper from a distance of around 30km.

That is just the start, however: even more impressive results will come when interferometers are launched into space. At present, the biggest telescope in space is the 2.5m Hubble Space Telescope – at 11 tons, the biggest the space shuttle could carry. Space interferometers will get around the weight problem by using an array of small mirrors. The Space Interferometry Mission (SIM), being launched in 2005, will produce images with four times the clarity of Hubble, while the telescope will weigh five times less. The Terrestrial Planet Finder (TPF), to be launched in 2011, will produce pictures 40 times clearer than Hubble's. Ultimately, the Planet Finder Device will comprise an array of TPF-class interferometers flying in formation, each carrying four 8m telescopes. That will be so powerful that it should be able to see planets orbiting other stars.

who was "skylab stan"?

After its third mission, the unoccupied Skylab drifted for five years and its orbit degraded. On 11 July 1979 it plunged into the atmosphere entirely out of control. Space officials crossed their fingers and hoped the debris would not fall on a populated area.

As it turned out, the craft disintegrated in the atmosphere high above the Nullarbor Plain in Western Australia. Some of the debris landed near a remote sheep station – Noodoonia – close to the small town of Balladonia, 850km east of Perth.

One piece of Skylab fell on to a golf course in Albany, Western Australia. At the time, there was a $10,000 reward on offer to the first person to retrieve a piece of the space station and take it back to the US. The winner was a teenage farm boy who had never before travelled outside his native Australia. He became popularly known as "Skylab Stan".

Backup procedures meant that Skylab wasn't the only space station in existence. In those days, NASA always built a duplicate spacecraft in case primary vehicles failed. Skylab was no exception. A complete copy of the Skylab space station, which was kept ready for flight, is now a permanent exhibit at the Smithsonian Air and Space Museum in Washington.

what are asteroids made of?

So far, only one probe has visited an asteroid – NASA's NEAR Shoemaker mission, which landed on the asteroid Eros in February 2001. Its gamma-ray instrument was able to analyse the surface, and confirm that the asteroid was a solid object rather than just a heap of rubble. But of course the NEAR Shoemaker findings apply only to Eros – and astronomers know that there are several different types of asteroid. Studies of the light reflected from asteroids by spectroscopy and polarisation have revealed that most are made of rather fragile carbonaceous material, while the majority of the rest contain at least some metal, notably iron. Analysis of radar signals bounced off asteroids suggests that some are pure metal.

This range of compositions initially led some astronomers to assume that the asteroids were once all part of a single, Earth-sized planet which was shattered by an impact early on in the history of the solar system. Released into space, material from the crust, mantle and core of this planet then spread out to form the asteroid belts.

Few astronomers still believe in the shattered planet idea, however. Instead, the asteroids are now thought to be rubble left over from the formation of the inner planets such as the Earth, with the action of Jupiter's gravity preventing the rubble from getting together to form a planet of its own. As such, asteroids are probably pristine remnants of the very oldest material in the solar system. They are also thought to be the source of many of the meteorites which land on the Earth, which have a similar chemical structure to the asteroids. The theory is that asteroids occasionally smash into one another, ejecting fragments that end up on Earth-crossing orbits and eventually hit the Earth. Just such a fragment, about the size of a house, struck Arizona around 49,000 years ago, creating the state's now famous Meteor Crater.

🪐 Is Pluto a planet?

🅰 The fact that hundreds of icy objects are known to occupy the outer Solar System has led some astronomers to believe that Pluto should be demoted from its planet status. The definition of a planet – a large object that orbits the Sun – is vague. For example, what does "large" mean when Pluto itself is smaller than Neptune's moon, Triton?

Myles Standish of NASA's Jet Propulsion Laboratory explains, "You have to draw the line somewhere. I would say that Pluto is large enough because if you line up the planets by size, when you get to the small guys: Mars, then Mercury, then Pluto, it's quite a big jump before you get to the largest asteroid, Ceres. So far as size goes, it is a natural boundary."

For those studying the Kuiper Belt, things seem different. "I always say that when we added the Kuiper Belt, we subtracted a planet!" says Dave Jewitt, Institute for Astronomy, Hawaii. "People say 'Oh you're demoting Pluto' but that's nonsense because Pluto is now the current king of the Kuiper Belt. That is a very good thing to be." The argument is bound to intensify if – or indeed when – other Pluto sized objects are found in the Kuiper Belt.

Jewitt says, "The main thing is it doesn't matter what you call these objects. The issue is to understand how they formed and what they tell us about the early history of the Solar System."

🪐 Does the sun have a sibling star?

🅰 Statistically, at least, it seems plausible: a recent study of over 100 sun-like stars in our cosmic neighbourhood revealed that over half were actually part of binary systems. In the late 1980s, a team of American astronomers proposed that the Sun might have a companion, which had so far escaped detection because it was a small, dim type of star known as a brown dwarf, following a huge, cigar-shaped orbit about the Sun. Taking around 26 million years to complete one orbit, the star would travel up to 150,000 astronomical units (AU – the distance between the Earth and the Sun) away from the solar system before slowly returning to come within 30,000 AU. The astronomers came up with this orbit because it offered an explanation of an apparently regular 26 million-year gap between mass extinctions of life on Earth. According to the astronomers, the star would drag comets off their orbits and send them hurtling towards us, where one such impact may have triggered the extinction of the dinosaurs.

Because of its destructive role, the star has been dubbed Nemesis (after the Greek goddess of retribution). Many astronomers are very sceptical of its existence, pointing out that the orbit of Nemesis is so long that the star could easily be wrenched from the Sun's grasp. Other researchers are sceptical about the reality of the 26 million-year period between extinctions – which rather undermines the reasons for postulating Nemesis in the first place. Even if it does exist, however, there's nothing to worry about for a while: it is probably at the very far end of its orbit, and thus won't be returning for a good 13 million years at least.

🞲 How long before Neil Armstrong's footprints on the moon finally wear away?

🞲 Along with six lunar modules and US flags, assorted scientific equipment and a plaque signed by Richard Nixon, the dozen astronauts who made it to the Moon between 1969 and 1972 peppered its surface with thousands of footprints. Incredibly, these apparently fragile indentations are actually more permanent than any man-made structure on Earth.

It is possible that many of the footprints were obliterated by the blast of the upper stage of the Lunar Module, as it took the astronauts back up into orbit. But for most, without wind or water to disturb them, there is no reason why – barring a freak meteoric impact – the footprints shouldn't remain intact for millions of years. What will eventually smooth them away (in an estimated 10 million years or so) will be the gentle downpour of micro-meteorites – cosmic particles less than 0.1mm across whose impact on the Moon over many aeons has chiselled away at its features.

when and where are the best times and places to see auroras?

In Britain, the further north you are, the better your chances: auroras are normally visible for more than 20 nights a year in the north of Scotland, compared with just a couple of nights a year in the South of England. But more important is the time that you go looking. Auroras are caused by fast-moving particles from the Sun smashing into molecules in the upper atmosphere, and so the more active the Sun, the more chance of seeing auroras. The Sun goes through a 11-year cycle of activity, which last reached a peak in 2000. This proved to be a good year for seeing auroras in Britain. Some of the best displays were seen between 9pm and midnight during the spring and autumn, when the orientation of the Earth's magnetic poles relative to the sun was most favourable.

During times of really violent solar activity, auroras can be seen more or less anywhere: in 1909 the Northern Lights were actually visible in Singapore – just a degree or so north of the Equator. For those not accustomed to seeing such phenomena, the results can be rather disconcerting. When the Northern Lights appeared over Italy during the first century AD, the Roman emperor Tiberius sent fire-fighters to the port of Ostia, fearing that the red glow visible over the area meant the harbour city was in flames.

when will we see a space plane?

Boeing is developing a 27ft winged spacecraft called the X-37 Advanced Technology Vehicle. The craft will be launched into orbit by a space shuttle and be able to re-enter Earth's atmosphere and land on a runway under its own power. In public, American officials say the little X-37 is being developed for NASA, but it's thought the military see it as a prototype for the Space Manoeuvre Vehicle (SMV) under consideration since the early 1990s. This secret craft would also be launched by a space shuttle and have a simple rocket engine and solar-electric cells to generate power to stay in orbit for months at a time.

If it is built, the SMV will roam space, monitoring Earth with surveillance gear, disabling enemy satellites and even firing lasers or kinetic weapons at Earth.

The US Air Force Scientific Advisory Board recommends that a final decision on the SMV should be made in about 2002, with a first demonstration flight around 2009 and an operational vehicle by 2015. If this happens, the SMV will be the first "space battleship".

Is there water in space?

Yes – and it may explain the origin of the Earth's oceans. Evidence for the existence of water elsewhere in the solar system has been steadily accumulating since the early 1970s. Vast, winding canyons on Mars suggest that rivers once flowed on that now-arid planet, while in 1999 NASA's Lunar Prospector spacecraft found signs of water ice at the north and south poles of the Moon (amounting to between 10 and 300 million tonnes of water spread over thousands of square miles).

But how did this water come to be there? One clue comes from studies of comets. Analysis of the light from Halley's comet has revealed that it spews out tens of tonnes of water every second as it approaches the sun. This has led some astronomers to speculate that the water in the solar system was dumped there by the torrent of comets believed to have rained down on the planets just after their formation around 4.5 billion years ago. If correct, this would mean that when we take a dip in the sea at Skegness, we're actually paddling in the remnants of comets that struck the Earth billions of years ago.

One scientist has gone further than this, however. Dr Louis Frank of Iowa University claims to have evidence that house-sized "mini-comets" still strike the upper atmosphere every few seconds, dumping yet more water into the Earth's oceans. Frank calculates that these mini-comets could account for all the water on Earth. Unfortunately for Frank, few scientists seem to agree. They argue that the tiny black dots seen on satellite images of the Earth are not mini-comets, as Frank believes, but just random noise.

Either way, it seems plausible that comets, at some point, have seeded our solar system with water.

🤖 what has the space programme done for us?

🤖 Ask people for an example of space programme spin-off, and it's a safe bet they'll come up with non-stick frying pans. In fact, Teflon was discovered almost 20 years before the flight of Sputnik 1, and kitchen utensils coated with it were on sale years before Armstrong made his giant leap for mankind.

Most of the spin-off from space technology is so fundamental that we take it more or less for granted. Satellite communications are a case in point. Weather forecasts are much more reliable because of the 24-hour monitoring of Earth's atmosphere made possible by satellites, and by giving early warnings of severe weather events like hurricanes, they have saved countless lives. The Global Positioning System would literally never have got off the ground were it not for the development of rockets that put satellites into space reliably and cheaply.

Then there's the computer. Until the space race, the typical computer was the size of a garage. NASA's demand for one small enough to go into space spurred the development of microchip technology now used in everything from personal organisers to mobile phones.

The scientists' desire to keep tabs on the physical condition of astronauts on their missions led to the development of the lightweight sensors you'll find on a hospital patient's body. Rechargeable pacemakers that regulate the heartbeat of cardiac patients and can be reprogrammed without extra surgery are another direct result of space spin-offs in micro-electronics and telemetry. And it's not just the US–Soviet space race that led to useful spin-offs. ABS anti-lock braking and air bags both rely on a deceleration sensor originally developed for the European space programme.

Despite these successes, it's far from clear that manned space exploration will continue to bring such impressive benefits. The International Space Station (ISS) has been touted as the likely birthplace of a host of breakthroughs in everything from medicine to metallurgy. But many experts are sceptical that the zero-gravity conditions aboard the ISS will prove to be of any great use to mankind.

The first spin-off product whose properties could only have been made in space was a polystyrene sphere created in the zero-gravity environment of the Space Shuttle, which can't be mimicked on Earth. Undistorted by gravity's pull, the sphere has very precise dimensions, making it useful for setting standards in manufacturing.

what was the worst ever rocket disaster?

Launching rockets is an inherently dangerous business which has claimed many lives. The most famous disaster was seen live on TV when on 28 January, 1996, seven astronauts died when the rocket-launched Space Shuttle Challenger was destroyed by a huge explosion seconds after lift-off. Yet most rocket disasters have happened in China and Russia over the years, where scientists have had to cut corners to meet deadlines.

China once hoped to monopolise the market for satellite-launchers, but is now shunned by many firms since two of its

"Long March" rockets blew up near the ground, killing more than 100 civilians. Most Soviet disasters were kept secret during the Cold War, but it is now known that in 1980, 50 Soviet technicians were killed when a booster rocket engine exploded while being fuelled.

The worst Soviet accident is thought to have happened in 1960, when Soviet leader Nikita Krushchev ordered a new rocket to be test-fired before it was ready. Marshal Mitrofan Nedelin, commander of Soviet Strategic Rocket Forces, and dozens of scientists, were incinerated at the launch pad when the rocket blew up. All that was left of the Marshal were his metallic medals.

what was the star of Bethlehem?

Everyone knows the biblical story of how the Three Wise Men followed a brilliant new star to Bethlehem and the birthplace of Christ. And over the years, a whole slew of theories have been put forward to explain the "star", from meteor showers to comets to conjunctions of the planets.

In 1954, the physicist and science fiction writer Arthur C. Clarke published an article arguing that the famed event may have been due to a supernova – the nuclear detonation of a supermassive star. But, if the "star" had been a supernova, it would have been seen by more than just wise men in Arabia: astronomers in China kept scrupulous accounts of events in the night sky for centuries before the birth of Christ.

In 1977, a study of celestial events recorded by Chinese astronomers revealed that between 10 March and 7 April in 5BC, they witnessed what they called a "Broom Star" near the constellation of Capricorn, which lingered in the area for 70 days before fading. The year and months fit extremely well with the timing of the birth of Christ as deduced by historians.

The problem with the supernova idea lies in that figure of 70 days. There is a connection between how bright a supernova is and how long it takes to fade, and for the "Christmas supernova" to have faded so quickly, the original explosion would have been pathetically dim, even at its brightest – and hardly worth chasing across Arabia. But the biggest blow to the supernova explanation is that astronomers have failed to find any signs of the remnants of a stellar explosion that might have taken place relatively near the Earth at around the time of the birth of Christ.

Arguably the best explanation put forward so far is that the Star of Bethlehem was a so-called "nova". Less spectacular than a supernova, a nova is triggered when hydrogen is dragged from one star onto another in orbit around it. Eventually enough hydrogen builds up to explode in a colossal thermonuclear blast, and the star brightens by a factor of 100,000 in just a few days.

The nova theory fits in well with both the Gospel accounts and the findings of modern physics. According to British astrophysicist Dr Mark Kidger, it is also backed by Chinese astronomical records, which seem to point to a nova explosion in the constellation Aquila in mid-March, 5BC.

what's the most likely site of life beyond the earth?

While Mars may once have sustained life, few scientists expect anything much to grow there now. As a site for currently-existing life beyond the Earth, at least as good a bet is Europa, one of the moons of Jupiter. On the face of it, this 2000-mile wide satellite would seem a pretty unlikely home for life: orbiting 490 million miles from the sun, it rarely gets above -100 °C out there. But data sent back by NASA's Galileo probe in 1995 suggests that Europa may have a vast ocean lurking under its ice-laden crust.

The water is kept above freezing by the constant wrenching at Europa by Jupiter's mighty gravitational field. By distorting the satellite, these so-called tidal forces are thought to be strong enough to keep temperatures under the ice-crust relatively balmy.

They might also trigger volcanic activity on Europa, similar to that already witnessed on Io, another moon of Jupiter. Such activity raises the possibility of primitive life existing near hydrothermal vents similar to those of the Earth's oceans, where undersea nutrients and warmth are supplied in lieu of sunlight.

To find out what is actually happening on Europa, NASA has plans to follow up the Galileo mission with a variety of probes, including the Europa Ice Clipper, which could return ice samples to Earth by the end of the decade.

🔵 what was the steady-state theory?

🔵 In 1948, the Cambridge mathematician Fred Hoyle, along with two university colleagues, put forward a radically new theory of the universe. Known as the Steady-state Theory, it argued that, instead of the universe exploding out of nowhere in a Big Bang billions of years ago, it has existed forever, with the matter we see around us steadily trickling into existence all the time.

Although an apparently outrageous idea, the Steady-state Theory turned out to be consistent with Einstein's theory of relativity and made clear predictions about what the universe must be like. During the 1950s and early 1960s, critics of the Steady-state Theory claimed to have proved these predictions wrong – though their supposed "proof" has since turned out to be less than convincing.

The real death-blow for the original Steady-state Theory came in 1965, when two US engineers discovered that the universe is filled with heat – exactly as expected if the universe had exploded into existence in a Big Bang (ironically, a term Hoyle himself coined as a joke). Ever since, most scientists have abandoned the Steady-state Theory in favour of the Big Bang.

However, during the past 20 years, evidence has emerged that Hoyle and his colleagues might have been closer to the truth than they imagined. In 1981, a possible explanation emerged for the Big

Bang, with sub-atomic effects in the very early universe triggering a rapid cosmic expansion called inflation. Intriguingly, the law governing this expansion was identical to the predictions of the Steady-state Theory.

New observations of the universe now also suggest that it will spend the rest of eternity expanding, according to the laws of the steady-state universe, propelled by the steady push of sub-atomic effects. Thus it may yet turn out that both theories are right, with the universe beginning with a Big Bang before settling into a steady state.

Did an eclipse really save christopher columbus' life?

Christopher Columbus' fourth voyage to the Americas was a disaster; he reached Jamaica with leaking ships and almost no food left. The natives refused to help him. But he knew a lunar eclipse would happen on 29 February 1504. Warning the natives in advance of the wrath of God, the eclipse hastily convinced them that he possessed god-like powers and they helped him.

A solar eclipse over Asia Minor on 25 May 585BC ended a battle between King Cyaxares of the Medes and King Alyattes of the Lydians. The two armies were so scared by the sudden darkness that they signed a peace treaty and went home. As this was the only eclipse in Asia Minor at that time, the battle is the first accurately dated historical event. That eclipse was also the first to be correctly predicted, by the Greek philosopher Thales. *The Gospel According to Luke* makes reference to what some have interpreted as an eclipse in Chapter 23, verses 44–45: "It was now the sixth hour, and there was a darkness over the whole land until the ninth hour, while the sun's light failed." But as the longest possible duration of totality for a solar eclipse is seven minutes and 31 seconds, this interpretation is thought by many to be more than a little unlikely.

when we see pictures taken on the moon's surface why are there no stars in the sky?

Perhaps the most telling evidence that the Moon landings weren't faked in a Los Angeles backlot is the distinctly black sky we see above Buzz Aldrin in the images from the lunar surface. What Hollywood movie producer could have resisted the temptation of adding a background of brilliant stars in contrast to a bleak moon set?

Incidentally, all but four Apollo 11 surface photos are of Buzz Aldrin – even the most famous one of all, showing the reflection of the photographer in the astronaut's gold visor. In their excitement the moonwalkers forgot to use their one Hasselblad 70mm camera to take more pictures of Neil Armstrong (again, taking just four pictures of the first man on the Moon is such a blunder you can't imagine hoaxers dreaming it up).

The moon has no atmosphere to limit the light coming down to its surface, so in theory there should be brilliant views of even the furthest stars. But the moonwalks all occurred during the lunar day. The glare of the unfiltered sun is considerable, so that all astronauts moonsuits were fitted with visors. The glare tended to mask the stars and this "washout" effect was made worse by reflected light from dust covering the lunar surface.

In fact, the lunar module's descent engines swept away all of the very fine surface dust, leaving larger, more jagged particles that were even better at reflecting light. As a result, from orbit, lunar landing sites would appear distinctively brighter than surrounding areas.

If an astronaut looked away from the sun into the darkest part of the sky, they could make out stars – but capturing images of stars requires long camera exposure times and the lunar photos were taken with exposure times too short to register them.

Still, the view during the lunar night, or from the dark side of the Moon, will always be awe-inspiring and it has been suggested that a large observatory be set up on the dark side some time later this century.

🔵 which man-made objects can you see from space?

🔵 From the edge of space – which officially begins at 100km from the Earth's surface – the unaided human eye can make out objects as small as 30 metres across. So contrary to popular belief, it's not possible to make out the Great Wall of China from orbit, let alone from the Moon, using only the naked eye: it's just not wide enough to see. That leaves plenty of other things that can be seen, however. There are many buildings and structures – from the Pentagon, home of the US Department of Defence, to Britain's own Millennium Dome – that are more than big enough to be seen from space.

Even with artificial aids, there are limits on what you can make out from space. The ultimate limit is set by the properties of light itself. These imply that – in theory, at least, – a 1-metre wide telescope could make out objects as small as 6cm from a height of 100km. US spy satellites, such as the Keyhole series, are said to be capable of this kind of performance already.

So much for theory: during the last Mercury spaceflight in May 1963, astronaut Gordon Cooper claimed to be able to see a vehicle on a road, and smoke trails from chimneys. Some people suggested that perhaps refraction by the atmosphere was making objects look larger – rather like objects in a glass of water look larger. Detailed calculations knocked this idea on the head, however; the magnification effect exists, but it's far too small to have any noticeable effect. It's much more likely that Cooper was just being fooled by his own eyes – though it has to be said that he was known to have phenomenally good eyesight, even by the impressive standards of the original astronaut corps.

Have astronauts ever seen UFOs in space?

There have been reports of mysterious objects by astronauts since the earliest days of space-flight. Two of the most puzzling occurred during NASA's Gemini programme of the 1960s. During the flight of Gemini 4 in June 1965, USAF Brigadier-General James McDivitt reported seeing a cylindrical object with what seemed to be antennas sticking out of it. When he and his co-pilot Edward White landed, their film was taken off them by officials. When the photos were released, they showed an object which McDivitt insisted was what he had seen. He believed he had seen some unmanned satellite, but no convincing identification of the object could be found among the tracking records of the US department of defence.

In December 1965, on board the Gemini 7 mission, USAF colonel Frank Borman told flight controllers in Houston that he could see another object orbiting in formation with his own craft. Again, obvious explanations – such as the object being part of Gemini 7's booster rocket – do not make sense. For a start, Borman and co-pilot James Lovell could see the booster as well. Secondly, the object seemed to be pursuing an orbit quite different from that followed by any components of Gemini 7.

Do astronauts get travel sickness?

Absolutely, for exactly the same reasons as on Earth – the conflict between what your eyes and inner ear are telling your brain about the position of your body. A travel-sick astronaut feels as though he's constantly falling. But a couple of anti-nausea tablets are even less efficient in stopping a rising urge to vomit on a space ship than they are on a cross-Channel ferry. Unfortunately, bilious astronauts can't take these or anything else. NASA doesn't allow its astronauts to pop any anti-sickness pills so that it can carry out research into space sickness. Unsurprisingly, this means that those with delicate stomachs are not the most popular of cabin mates in zero gravity.

🔵 Does space get warmer closer to the Big Bang?

🔴 The short answer is yes. The Big Bang engulfed the entire cosmos around 15 billion years ago, and the resulting heat has been fading away ever since. It's now around 3°C above Absolute Zero – that is, a rather chilly -270°C.

According to the Big Bang theory, galaxies billions of light years away are also immersed in space that is billions of years closer in time to the cataclysmic explosion of the Big Bang. So if that theory is right, space should have been slightly warmer back then – and by an amount that can be calculated exactly using equations derived from the theory.

In December 2000, an international team of astronomers announced that it had succeeded in measuring the temperature of space around a galaxy so distant that its light comes from just three billion years after the Big Bang. The team did it by studying light from molecules of gas agitated by the heat from the primordial explosion, and this revealed that the temperature of space back then was between 6 and 14 degrees above Absolute Zero – still incredibly cold, but somewhat warmer than today's 3 degrees above. It's also right in line with calculations of what the temperature should have been according to Big Bang theory, which predicts 9 degrees.

🔵 Why does the moon seem a long way away at some times, but much larger and closer at others?

🔴 Every now and then, instead of being its normal, modestly proportioned self, the Moon appears to swell up to an enormous orb that seems to fill half the sky and appears so close you could almost touch it. This is not because the Moon is any closer to the Earth, or even the result of some bizarre atmospheric effect. It is in fact a simple optical illusion. It occurs only when the Moon is near the horizon, where the eye sees it next to objects on the ground. When it's high up, there's no yardstick by which to compare it. But at the horizon the Moon suddenly seems very big next to buildings, trees and roads. This effect is further compounded by the fact that our brains are used to seeing things we know to be very big (skyscrapers, for example) looking very small when they're far off on the horizon. When the Moon appears over the top of these objects looking bigger than them, your brain "assumes" it must be absolutely monstrously huge – and the brain compensates for this confusing visual information by greatly inflating the Moon's apparent size.

can you put the science of a wormhole into layman's terms?

The ideas that space is riddled with wormholes connecting different parts of the cosmos is older than you might think. A German physicist named Ludwig Flamm first raised the possibility in 1915. He based his ideas on Einstein's general theory of relativity, published the same year.

According to Flamm, matter warps space and time around it, like a finger poked against a balloon warps its surface. If you poke hard enough, one side will touch the other, forming a tunnel through four-dimensional spacetime. While no-one has yet found a way of making one, no-one has proved it to be an impossible task either.

Are there any ways of getting into space that don't involve rockets?

NASA is keenly looking for alternative ways of getting into orbit as the current method of space travel is extremely expensive. Magnetic levitation technology (maglev) could be the answer to reducing this cost.

Maglev currently works using magnetised coils that run along the train track and repel same-charge magnets on the undercarriage of the train producing levitation of 1–10cm. Once in the air, AC electric power supplied to the coils causes reversals of charge. Consequently, a system of same-charge and opposite-charge forces push and pull the train along the line.

The initial launch of a rocket is the most costly part because of the amount of fuel required. Maglev would slash this expense because it would be ground-based and require virtually no fuel for lift-off. The economy of the system is further enhanced because it has no moving parts and, as a result, is practically maintenance free. Unlike boosters, maglev is re-usable (perhaps for up to 30 years). Working in the same fashion as the tracks that power trains, the maglev track would propel the craft to 600mph, when the boosters would kick in to take the rocket into orbit. NASA officials have plans to have maglev systems operational within the next decade. If that happens, maglev could then make space travel cheap enough to make the moon a possible holiday destination.

Another method is even simpler: the Space Elevator. First dreamed up by a Russian schoolteacher called Konstantin Tsiolkovski (who, ironically enough, is now regarded as the father of rocketry), the idea involves connecting a cable from the ground up to an orbiting "anchor point". Elevator cars could then travel up and down the cable, which would be kept taut by the momentum of the orbiting anchor.

A recent NASA report has suggested that such an elevator may be a realistic possibility. It talks of electromagnetically-propelled elevator cars zipping up and down a 22,000-mile long cable, with a small asteroid brought into Earth orbit acting as counterweight. Crucially, new materials discovered in the 1990s known as carbon nanotubes seem able to cope with the incredibly high cable tensions which would be created.

Arthur C. Clarke, who mentioned the Space Elevator idea in his

1979 novel Fountains of Paradise, has already made his prediction of when we'll be able to just catch a lift up into space: "The space elevator", he says, "Will be built about 50 years after everyone stops laughing."

🔵 what will happen when the sun burns out?

🔵 Around five billion years from now, the Sun's core will begin to run out of the hydrogen fuel needed to keep it burning, and it will start to shrink. As it does so, it will release energy into the rest of the sun, which will start to heat up and expand. After just a few million years, the sun will have ballooned into a huge "red giant" star so big that it will engulf the orbit of the Earth, wiping out all life. At the same time, the sun's core will have shrunk to around just 2 per cent of its original size, becoming so hot that it triggers so-called helium burning. This will cause the Sun to expand even further, right out beyond the orbit of Mars, becoming a red supergiant. Further nuclear reactions will then trigger a series of detonations to tear through the dying Sun, stripping the core of its surrounding material, which will be blown off like a smoke ring, forming a so-called planetary nebula. The core will then settle down to form an extremely hot, dense "white dwarf" star which will slowly cool and dim.

🔵 why does the moon go red during a lunar eclipse?

🔵 During a lunar eclipse, the Earth comes between the Sun and the Moon, cutting off a lot of the sunlight that normally reaches it. A lot, but not all: some sunlight still gets through by being bent by the Earth's atmosphere, and scattered by the dust particles in it. The longer the wavelength of light, the less it is scattered, so it's the long-wavelength red component of sunlight that tends to get through unscathed and reach the Moon – giving it a spectacular red tinge. Quite how spectacular depends on how much dust there is in the Earth's atmosphere. If the atmosphere is relatively clean, the eclipse will appear a vivid red-orange. But during the eclipse of 30 December 1963, the moon almost disappeared from view. Virtually all of the sunlight was blotted out by volcanic dust injected into the atmosphere by the eruption of Mt Agung in Bali.

How fast does the earth spin and will it ever stop spinning?

Our planet has an equatorial diameter of 12,756km, and takes 23 hours, 56 minutes to perform one complete rotation. So at the equator it's spinning at around 1,700km per hour – so fast, that the resulting centrifugal force reduces the effect of gravity. Weight-watchers need not get very excited, though: for a 10-stone person, the reduction amounts to about half a pound. Equatorial spin is fast enough to cause a distortion in the size of the Earth, making it fatter at the equator by around 42km.

The Earth's rotation is slowing down, however – mainly because of the effect of the Moon on the oceans. Friction generated by the dragging of trillions of tons of water over the world's beaches with every tide helps add about 1.5 seconds to every day per 100,000 years.

As the current day is 86,164 seconds long, the Earth will finally come to a grinding halt about five billion years from now. But don't worry about the working day literally dragging on forever – the Sun is expected to run out of fuel about then, so you won't be able to see what you're doing anyway.

How long would it take to visit every galaxy?

In 1995, scientists working with the Hubble Space Telescope found there were at least 10 billion galaxies in the visible universe. As the universe is around 12 billion light years across, that means there's roughly 5 million light-years of empty space between each one. So even travelling at the speed of light, it's going to take several tens of millions of billions of years to get around to visiting each one. Put another way, even if the Starship *Enterprise* could visit galaxies at the rate of one per daily episode of *Star Trek*, it would still take 27 million years to get around to seeing them all. Even the most hardened Trekkie might get a bit fed up before then.

🤖 is it possible to see orbiting satellites from earth?

🤖 Yes – because although they're relatively small, they reflect a lot of sunlight. The best way to find them is by looking towards the south during the night (most satellites orbit the equator of the Earth, and the equator is south of the UK). Unlike aircraft, which have coloured flashing lights at night, satellites appear as fairly bright white or yellow "stars" moving across the sky, usually from east to west or vice versa (those that travel from north to south are survey satellites – including spy satellites). The speed of movement of satellites is another tell-tale sign; taking at least 90 minutes to travel around the globe, they'll cover around 4 degrees in a minute – which is equivalent to the angle subtended by the width of your thumb held at arm's length in around 8 seconds.

🤖 why does the lunar surface always have the same appearance?

🤖 In fact, the Moon doesn't always look exactly the same. Although it always keeps the same face towards Earth, we actually see 59 per cent of it over the course of a year. This is because wobbling effects, called librations, give us an angular peek around the far side. About 41 per cent is visible all the time, 41 per cent is always hidden and 18 per cent swings in and out of view.

🔹 If the sun vanished right now, how long would it take before we'd know?

🔹 We'd realise that our source of light and its gravitational field had vanished at the same time, as both light and gravity travel at a speed of around 300,000km per second. So, with our distance from the Sun being around 150 million kilometres, we'd learn the awful truth about 500 seconds, or 8 minutes and 20 seconds after it happened.

🔹 Does anyone own the moon?

🔹 Ever since Neil Armstrong and his space-suited chums started cavorting on the Moon, there has been a popular misconception that it is actually the property of the United States.

"Because the Apollo astronauts planted flags in the moon, a lot of people seriously think America owns it," says Trevor Raggatt of the British National Space Centre.

In fact, those TV-friendly Stars and Stripes, many of which are said to have been blown over by the blast of the astronauts leaving the lunar surface, never possessed more than symbolic importance anyway. "The issue of space ownership was actually settled by an international treaty in 1968," says Raggatt.

UN Treaty Series Number 10, entitled "Treaty on Principles Governing the Action of States in the Exploration and Use of Outer Space, including the Moon and other Celestial Bodies", deals specifically with the subject. Article Two declares: "Outer space ... is not subject to national appropriation by claims of sovereignty by means of use or occupation or by any other means."

As with Antarctica, designated a "world park", the Moon and the rest of outer space belong to everybody and nobody.

why is it dark at night?

If you think it's because the part of the Earth you are on is turned away from the Sun, then think again: that doesn't actually explain why space itself is dark. And as the German astronomer Heinrich Olbers pointed out over 150 years ago, there are very good reasons for believing that space should actually be incredibly bright. That's because although the glow from stars becomes fainter the more distant they are, the number of stars enclosed in this ever-greater volume of space increases – and the two effects should exactly cancel each other out. Extended right out into the infinite universe, that means that the night sky should actually be blindingly bright.

So why isn't it? Olbers himself thought that interstellar dust would block the light from the most distant stars. The trouble with that solution is that this dust would steadily heat up until it too shone as brightly as the stars behind it.

Another way out of Olbers' Paradox, as it became known, emerged after astronomers discovered that the universe is expanding. The more distant the galaxies, the faster they appear to recede from the Earth. At some point, therefore, galaxies must be so far away – and moving so rapidly – that their light never catches up with us to add to the brightness of the night sky.

In fact, the expansion effect cannot resolve the paradox either – the rate of expansion is simply too slow to have the required diluting effect. Astronomers now believe that there is no one, single reason for why the sky is dark at night. The most important factor is that the universe is still relatively young and filled with stars that have only relatively recently started to shine. As a result, these stars simply haven't had time to fill the expanding universe with their glow. Yet even billions of years from now, their contribution won't add up to much, as they are too small and widely-separated to lead to a brilliant night sky.

astronauts, telescopes and the universe

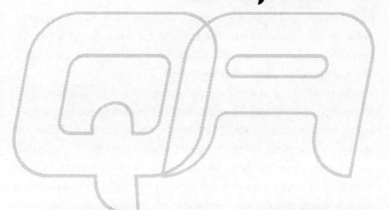

the Human

the Human

Body

Body

will cloning make fingerprinting useless?

Even cloned human beings would have different fingerprints, because the characteristic patterns aren't totally dictated by genetics – which explains why identical twins, who share the same DNA, don't have identical fingerprints.

Quite what makes fingerprints unique is, however, still something of a mystery. The answer probably lies in the way the so-called friction ridges making up the prints are formed. There are around 400 of these ridges for every square centimetre of friction skin (which occurs on the palms of the hands and the undersides of thumbs and fingers) and their shape is influenced by the shape of the surface they grow on. Swellings called volar pads develop on the ridges. The size and shape of these pads seems to be partly inherited: closely related people often have similar patterns. But other – possibly random – factors are also important. These include the way the biochemicals needed to form skin combine in different concentrations at different points on the finger-tips.

Some people are born without real prints. Children with Down's Syndrome don't have complete ridges as such because of a flaw in embryonic development. There is also a very rare skin disease which causes people to be born without ridges on their friction skin.

First introduced in India in 1870 as a means of identification, fingerprinting was put on a scientific basis in 1892 by the great English anthropologist Sir Francis Galton, whose classification method is still used today. Galton was also the first person to attempt to calculate the likelihood of two fingerprints matching by chance alone; his estimate of around one in 70 billion is still regarded as reliable today.

The biggest threat to the use of prints to solve crimes was the discovery, in 1958 by a New Orleans dermatologist, that prints can be obliterated by the kind of clinical abrasion used to remove severe facial blemishes.

How do sperm move and how do they locate the egg?

Sperm have a simple design. The genetic material is carried in the head region while the tail propels the sperm. Behind the head is an area densely packed with mitochondria – energy generators – for propulsion. The tail contains microtubules – rod-like structures – along its length. Between these are small arms made of the protein dyenin which slide the microtubules past each other. This movement gives the tail a whip-like action, pushing the sperm forward.

The sperm of sea urchins are directed to the eggs by a chemical attractant and scientists have tried to discover if a similar mechanism exists in mammals. But after release, mammalian sperm can be found in both fallopian tubes, indicating that they move in a random direction, without guidance.

Why do teeth have nerves – and why can't you transplant them?

The nerves in teeth aren't there just to give you a hard time at the dentist – they're often what told you that a trip to the dentist was necessary in the first place. They're crucial for keeping a check on the state of your teeth, and routinely give feedback on temperature and bite pressure. By letting you know the consistency of the food in your mouth, they tell you when you can stop chewing – which is pretty useful if you don't want to choke. Nerves can even help teeth self-repair after injury, allowing the pulp region to retreat further down into the tooth, laying down hard layers above it. Sadly, however, this doesn't happen after common tooth decay.

There's no reason why teeth transplants can't be used as an alternative to dentures, and they were popular with rich Victorians. However, the high infection risk and low success rate makes them a risky option. Titanium tooth implants are sometimes used, with the implant being screwed into the patient's jaw, where the bone grows around it, giving a nice snug fit. A metal tooth-like covering is then fitted on top. The only problem is that each tooth costs hundreds of pounds and there's no discount given for bulk.

How much of my body could I live without?

A surprisingly large amount; the human body has a lot of built-in redundancy, says Timothy Davidson of the Department of Surgery, University College London. You can get by without spleen, appendix or gall bladder and you can lose one of your kidneys, and three of your four parathyroid glands. Three-quarters of the thyroid and liver can be removed without any serious consequences. However, although surgeons can remove your thyroid, adrenal glands and pancreas, they have to provide you with replacement hormone therapy for the rest of your life.

The gut is basically a tube running from the mouth to the anus. Much of it can be removed: the whole of the colon, for instance, the stomach, and several feet of small intestine. But depending on the extent of the operation the patient may need to be tube fed, which naturally affects quality of life.

The sexual organs – womb, ovaries, breasts, testes and penis – can be removed (and often are because of cancer) without affecting survival at all.

In fact, the only absolutely essential organs are the heart, lungs and brain, although the heart and lungs can be replaced temporarily by a machine or permanently by donor organs. People can and do also survive the removal of bits of brain – after operations on tumours, for example, or after injury – although they can suffer loss of function as a result.

There is one person in the UK and a few in the US who have lost all four limbs. Interestingly, for those doing the calculations, any amputation will shorten your life expectancy by around five years, regardless of what the limb is and whether it's replaced or not.

Ⓠ can we keep getting taller, faster and stronger, or is there a natural limit?

Ⓐ Although human beings are getting taller now, this hasn't always been the case. The height of our ancestors *Homo habilis* and *erectus* did increase steadily until 200,000 years ago. Then, for reasons we do not understand, it began to fall off again. Five thousand years ago, the trend was again reversed. This time the increase was due to better nutrition.

In the UK, adult height has been increasing by six to seven millimetres per generation for the last 30 years, an increase that is now levelling off. In developing countries height is increasing faster than it is in this country. But there is a maximum height for humans, and it is set by the fact that as bipedal creatures we are inherently unstable. Above a certain height, every time we fell over we would be at grave risk of lethal head injury.

It is possible to calculate the maximum safe height humans could routinely grow to, and it comes out at around 3 metres; interestingly, even the tallest-ever human, Robert Wadlow (1918-1940), was – at 2.72m – well within this maximum limit.

As we get bigger, we get faster and stronger too. Records are still being broken, but the rate is slowing. For instance, the record time for the one hundred metres was 10.2 seconds in 1953; Leroy Burrell bought it down to 9.85 seconds in 1994, but that was only one hundredth of a second less than the time that Carl Lewis set in 1991. Any new sporting records these days owe more to improvements in equipment, training techniques, diet and psychology than to improvements in the performance of the human machine.

Ⓠ can you predetermine your child's sex?

Ⓐ There are three schools of thought on this, without resorting to tampering with sperm. Professor Stolkowshi's diet method states that women who want to increase their chances of conceiving a boy should eat a diet rich in sodium and potassium (salty foods, white bread, pasta, rice, fresh fruit and vegetables). Those who want a girl should stick to a diet rich in calcium and magnesium and low in salt (milk, fresh cream, yoghurt, and only a little meat or fish).

French scientist Patrick Schoun believes that timing is everything. For a fee he will work out a lovemaking calendar based on the woman's polarity cycle. According to his research, the human ovum carries an electrical charge, either positive or negative, which changes during the fertile period. A positively charged egg attracts "X" sperm, giving a baby girl, whereas a negatively charged egg attracts "Y" sperm, producing a boy.

A certain Dr Jonus from the Czech Republic says women have two periods of fertility every month: the well-known biological menstrual cycle, and a second, rather less well-known one, which he claims, is controlled by the gravitational effects of the moon in relation to the sun at the time the child is born.

why do football referees make so many mistakes?

Research suggests that referees and their assistants get about one in five offside decisions wrong. But those who think they can do better should bear in mind the results of scientific research that shows that it's all but impossible for human referees to get every such decision right. One problem is that it takes up to 0.3 seconds for the eye to bring visual signals to a focus – by which time the players will have moved on a few metres, making any off-side decision instantly out of date.

Scientists at the Free University of Amsterdam, Holland, have also discovered that unless officials are exactly in line with the players involved in an offside decision, they are likely to fall victim to an optical illusion. To see what they mean, take a couple of pens and hold them upright in each hand. Now line the pens up at arm's

chapter 2

40

length, so that one is hidden behind the other. Imagine that the hidden pen is Attacker X on a run from left to right, and the pen closer to you is Defender Y, trying the offside trap. From where you're looking at them now, both players are in line, and so Attacker X is on side. But keeping the two pens stationary, just move your head slightly to the right. As you see it, Attacker X now appears to be the right of Defender Y – that is, closer to the goal line. Of course, he's really still in line with the defender – yet he appears to be just offside. With such optical tricks at work, the wonder is that more wrong decisions aren't made.

(Q) what's the loudest noise made by a human?

(A) You may be forgiven for thinking that a regimental sergeant major would be about the noisiest person around, but the record for the world's loudest shout is actually held by the sylph-like Annalisa Wray from Belfast, whose recorded shout in 1994 measured an astounding 121.7 decibels (dB), which is 20 times noisier than most people can manage (around 100 dB). Only one person has ever made a louder noise: Simon Robinson from Australia who, in 1988, recorded a scream of 128 dB. By comparison, an average conversation measures 50 dB, a busy street 70 dB, and heavy machinery 90 dB. Scarily, our record-holders are starting to compete with jet aircraft.

The decibel scale measures the power packed into the sound waves not their frequency. It is therefore linked to the sheer energy with which a person's lungs expel air through his or her vocal chords. The size of a pair of lungs and the sex of their owner are therefore less significant than their physical strength.

Prolonged noise above 150 dB will cause permanent deafness in the listener. Sound levels above 90 dB are generally illegal in factories in the western world, but that doesn't stop us choosing to give our ears a sonic mugging. Personal stereos are capable of piping upwards of 125 dB into your head.

ⓠ why do hair and nails keep on growing, even after death?

ⓐ When a person dies, some of the normal activities of their cells may take a few hours to stop completely. So hair and nails can still be produced during that short period of time. However, hair and nails grow so slowly that you would not be able to measure this brief post-mortem continuation of growth.

There is a common – and incorrect – belief that hair and nails continue to grow for much longer than this after death, perhaps because they are both formed from "dead" material. Nails are made of a tough protein called keratin, while hair is made of dead keratin-containing cells with varying amounts of pigment.

The skin on a corpse starts to shrink and it is this that gives the illusion that the hair and nails are longer than they were at death.

ⓠ why is it that when I go out in the sun, I sneeze – and then everything looks yellow?

ⓐ These two phenomena are not strictly linked, though there is an interrelation between eyes, sneezing and strong sunlight. The normal reason for sneezing is irritation of the nasal passages, which stimulates the trigeminal nerve running through the face and into the brain. Impulses from the trigeminal nerve end up in the respiratory centre of the medulla at the top of the spinal cord and trigger the sneeze impulse – with luck expelling whatever caused the irritation in the first place.

But the trigeminal nerve also serves the eye – whenever you sneeze, you also blink. When you step into bright sunshine, your eye reacts to the increased light input by blinking and contracting the pupils. This reaction is picked up by the trigeminal nerve and may produce a sneeze. Sunlight bleaches the pigments in the retina which see colour. It takes up to 20 minutes for the pigments to recover from this, and as each one returns to its normal state, you seem to see the corresponding colour at the expense of the others. Some people don't see yellow after adjusting to strong sun, but red or green. It all depends on the make-up of the individual eyes.

(Q) The TV show said $6 million, but how much would a bionic man really cost to "rebuild"?

(A) The body's basic functions – breathing, blood purification and so on – can be pretty well done by heart-lung, kidney dialysis and blood toxin-screening machines. One of each of these, plus a set of the very latest prosthetic limbs, an artificial heart and supporting hardware adds up to a very reasonable £200,000.

At present, we can't replicate the "thinking power" of the brain – a standard PC has nowhere near the power to copy even its most basic operations. Other human functions which we can't copy artificially include digestion, immune responses and the ability to reproduce. But we do have the artificial nose, cochlea implants for the ear and artificial mouths, which can chemically analyse "taste".

If all these could be fitted together to make a rather bizarre human robot, the cost would be only just over £300,000 which, even when you take into account today's value of the pound against the dollar, is nowhere near $6 million.

(Q) What is the composition of the air you breathe out?

(A) The main difference between inhaled and exhaled air lies in its oxygen and carbon dioxide content. The air that we all breathe is composed of 79 per cent nitrogen, 20.9 per cent oxygen and 0.04 per cent carbon dioxide, with traces of water vapour, rare gases and various pollutants.

Exhaled air is 16 per cent oxygen and 4 per cent carbon dioxide – the waste product of cellular respiration. Though it's absorbed by the body, nitrogen is not metabolised and is breathed in and out in the same quantity. Exhaled air also contains water picked up from the moist lining of the air tubes in the lungs, and is at body temperature rather than the temperature of the surrounding atmosphere.

Exhaled breath can be used for diagnostic purposes. A fruity smell can be a sign of impending diabetic coma, while bacteria involved in lung, mouth and gut infections may give off volatile compounds that make the breath smell bad.

A particularly useful breath test is for the stomach bug, *Heliobacter pylori*, which causes ulcers and increases the risk of gastric cancer. *Heliobacter* possesses an enzyme called urease, which enables it to survive the acid conditions of the stomach. Urease creates carbon dioxide as a by-product and this can be detected in the breath of an infected person. As analytical techniques become more sensitive, researchers believe that we may be able to use the breath test to diagnose many other diseases, such as cancers.

🖭 You can transplant hearts, but could you transplant a womb into a man?

🖭 The first challenge is to consider what you currently get in a male-to-female sex change operation: a vagina whose lining is created from the inwardly turned skin of the penis (the original "filling" of which is removed, along with the testes). Transsexuals push the process further with sex hormone therapy which helps breasts grow and modifies body shape.

Some male-to-female transsexuals would like to become women in the fullest sense of the word and bear their own children with a transplanted womb. Unfortunately, it's not practically possible now, nor will it be in the foreseeable future, according to Tim Jones, a spokesman for the UK's main centre for sex-change surgery – Charing Cross Hospital.

Assuming you could get a donor, there would be the usual rejection problems that you get in transplant operations. On top of that, a man hasn't room in his abdominal cavity for a womb anyway. And even if you could find enough space, you've still got to plumb in ovaries, Fallopian tubes, and if you actually want the system to function get the brain to pump out the appropriate hormones at the right time to drive the menstrual cycle. As someone asked in Monty Python's *Life of Brian*, "Where's the foetus going to gestate, then, in a box?"

can eunuchs have sex?

Yes, they can. Castration – in general, taken to mean the removal of the testes – does not render the penis unusable. Eunuchs can have erections and orgasms (although they can't produce sperm). However, in India, where eunuchs are sacred, men have their penises as well as their testes cut off in an operation that involves lopping off the whole ensemble with a knife. Deaths are common: lucky survivors report bleeding and extreme pain.

is there a scale for measuring pain, and what condition gives the greatest pain?

There is a scale, but it's based on a patient questionnaire, rather than an objective measurement like a blood test. It is called the McGill Questionnaire and consists of a series of descriptive words read out to someone who is in pain. Each set of 3-6 words has a ranking of one (low) to 20 (high). The overall score is a sum of all the words used. For instance, the word "throbbing" has a low ranking of 1, while "agonising" has the highest ranking of 20. The best way of using McGill is to calculate the Present Pain Index, where pain is classified as: 1=mild, 2=discomforting, 3=distressing, 4=horrible, 5=excruciating. The McGill questionnaire defines eight basic types of pain based on the descriptive words used. The categories are: neuralgia after shingles, phantom limb pain, cancer pain, tooth ache, certain forms of backache, arthritis, labour pain, and period pain.

As for which is the most painful experience, experts in analgesia (the relief of pain) point out that this will vary from person to person. For example, while around 40 per cent of women find childbirth moderately painful, a quarter find it excruciating. And plenty of soldiers have had limbs blown off, but not felt a thing for hours. Many doctors reckon the pain most likely to bring even the toughest to their knees is due to renal calculi: "kidney stones". Made from a build-up of salts in the kidney, the stones cause pain when they start to move into the bladder, their razor-sharp edges slashing through tissue on the way. The pain is so bad that victims feel like they are being stabbed to death, and the only relief comes when doctors deliver a knockout injection of morphine.

How rare is perfect pitch?

Absolute or "perfect" pitch is the ability to identify one note on the musical scale heard in isolation. It is thought to be a very rare trait and one that very few people possess. Indeed, much more common is relative pitch, the knowledge of the difference between two notes.

Theories abound on whether absolute pitch (AP) can be taught or whether it is in the genetic make-up of only a select few. However, a recent report suggests that AP may not be as rare as we in the West like to think. US psychologist Diana Deutsch believes that AP may be quite common, especially among people who speak tonal languages such as Mandarin. She argues that since sound variations form an integral part of their native languages, they therefore associate different notes with words. This research would suggest that AP is a trait that can be acquired as we learn.

How long can a human hold their breath for?

The Guinness Book of Records states that Robert Foster held his breath under 10ft of water for a record 13 minutes 42.5 seconds (after hyperventilating on oxygen for 30 minutes). However, the longest anyone has ever held their breath during underwater diving is 2 minutes 43 seconds. Under normal circumstances, the brain decides how long you can hold your breath for. Carbon dioxide is the waste product of respiration. When this builds up in the blood, it is a sign that more oxygen is needed fast. Carbon dioxide dissolves to form carbonic acid in the blood. This passes through the blood-brain barrier, and respiratory neurons in the medulla – part of the brain stem – respond to the increasing acid levels by triggering another breathing action.

You can override this automatic mechanism and hold your breath as a voluntary act. This involves neurons in the brain's outer layer – the cortex. Breath control is vital in singing, swimming, diving and yoga. Toddlers often indulge in breath holding to frighten their parents and get attention. However, the medullary reflexes will always eventually overcome any attempts at voluntary breath holding.

Crocodiles are able to stay up to an hour underwater without surfacing for air, simply because their haemoglobin is better at holding oxygen than ours. Scientists at Cambridge University are researching "improved" haemoglobin that incorporates this genetic trait as a possible tool for treating human blood diseases.

can women with implants still breast-feed?

This question is coming up more and more as increasing numbers of women opt for breast enhancement. So far, more than a million women have had silicone implants to increase the size of their breasts. Many did not think about breast-feeding at the time of the operation, because they were not planning to have a family.

The short answer to this question is, it depends on how the surgeon has done the operation. If the milk ducts that lead to the nipple are severed or blocked then breast-feeding is out. The same is true if the nerve or blood supply to the nipple has been affected by the surgery. However, in other cases, breast feeding with an implant should be possible.

Many women report problems such as blocked milk ducts and abscesses after breast operations of all kinds – not just cosmetic surgery. However, loss of sensation around the nipple often occurs with implants. This can lead to interference with the operation of the hormones prolactin and oxytocin, which are both involved in milk production. Some women have implants in just one breast to remedy a lopsided look. In these cases there should be no problem in feeding with the unaffected breast.

There have been scare stories about implants, but the good news is that they do not deteriorate as you get older and they don't suddenly explode if you go up in an aircraft.

why do middle-aged men lose hair on top, while it gets thicker and darker elsewhere?

Forty per cent of all men have lost some of the hair from the temples and crown of their heads by the time they are 35. The commonest type of baldness – male pattern baldness – is hereditary. If your father lost most of his hair by age 40, your chances of having a full head of hair at that age are slim.

The growth of hair is regulated by hormones. At adolescence, boys start growing darker, coarser hair on the face, chest and abdomen as a result of a surge in production of the male hormone testosterone. In middle age, high levels of testosterone can cause body hair to become thicker and darker but cause scalp hair to thin. So balding men are in a sense more "manly". No one knows exactly why these effects have evolved, or whether they have any evolutionary advantages.

could I catch a disease from someone who died several centuries ago?

Today, most deaths in the UK are due to non-infectious diseases. However, in previous centuries many people died from infectious diseases such as plague, cholera, typhoid, tuberculosis, anthrax and smallpox.

"The organisms that cause the first four do not survive well outside their living host," explains a spokesperson for the Public Health Laboratory Service, "but the risks presented by anthrax and smallpox are less clear."

Anthrax can form highly resistant spores that can last for long periods in dry conditions, while the smallpox virus in scabs has been shown to survive for at least 13 years in a laboratory cupboard. The orthopox virus, closely related to the smallpox virus, was seen on bodies more than 100 years old found in a London crypt in 1985.

The PHLS has not ruled out the possibility that someone could catch a disease from a person who died centuries earlier, and advises that anyone who excavates crypts should be vaccinated as a precaution. They also point out that inhalation hazards associated with digging up dead bodies are likely to be greater in crypts than in the open air.

what gives people naturally curly hair?

Blame it on your parents. There's no miracle cure for making curly hair straight or vice versa because, like hair colour, the shape of your hair is genetic. In general, the straighter and rounder the hair follicle, the straighter the hair.

Unfortunately for the frizz-heads among us, straight hair is stronger and a lot more weather resistant. Exposure to the elements is likely to have an instant "just-put-my-finger-in-the-socket" effect. Seawater, the chlorine in your local swimming pool and even shampooing all have the same effect. And for the helical-shaped curl, just pulling a comb through your hair is enough to traumatise it, according to John Fimage of the Scalp and Hair Clinic. Luckily, hair is a mass of dead protein, so you can always cut it all off and start again.

what is pins and needles?

The tingling sensation known as pins and kneedles is caused by a reaction from the nervous system to less than normal levels of blood flowing through the arteries in a limb. When we move into a better position, the pins and needles will continue for the time that it takes the body to correct the blood flow.

In some cases, the compression which causes the sensation can take place directly on a length of nerve, and then become chronic; a condition that's known as neuropathy. In other cases, the same sensation can be provoked by substances that affect the nervous system, such as alcohol or cocaine.

can you remove tattoos without leaving scars?

Yes. While older tattoo-removal techniques stripped away layers of skin with your tattoo, the lasers used today emit a wavelength of light that passes through the skin but is still absorbed by the tattoo ink. This rapid absorption of laser energy causes the ink to break down, and the tattoo is then removed by the body's normal filtering systems. The latest gadgets in the laser range are the "Medlite Q-Switched Nd-YAG" (try saying that in a hurry!), the Alexandrite and the Q-switch Ruby lasers. These deliver short, high-intensity pulses for maximum ink destruction.

The modern laser removal process does leave some pinpoint bleeding and is not totally painless – the effect of the laser pulse has been compared to the sensation of a speck of boiling fat on the skin – though most patients won't need anaesthetic for the procedure.

Three or four sessions are needed for removing an amateur tattoo, and five or six for a professional one. These treatments must be at least a month apart. Some colours, such as black, blue and red, are more easily destroyed than others. Green and yellow ink are hardest to remove.

🔵 In the TV series The Prisoner, villagers are often made instantly unconscious with "sleep gas". Is this possible?

🔴 In short, no it isn't – asphyxiating people is far easier than just knocking them out for a while. Anaesthesia is a very tricky and precise procedure; delivering the right amount is far from easy, with liquid anaesthetics such as ether and chloroform being highly volatile. The only gaseous option, nitrous oxide (laughing gas, N_2O), is also less than perfect, requiring a lot to knock somebody out, rather than simply leaving them falling around laughing. Worse still, as both sides discovered in World War I, gas can be a very fickle way of subduing people. There were several instances of sudden changes of wind blowing lethal gas away from the enemy and back into the faces of those who had unleashed it.

🔵 Why do we get bags under our eyes when we are tired?

🔴 When we are tired – or ill – tiny blood vessels beneath the eye tend to expand. It's a typical response to stress – from infection to injury. Oxygen-carrying blood, together with substances that help combat stresses, pass through these dilated vessels, bringing more fluid to the area under the eye. This creates puffiness, which looks like "bags" of flesh. Because the skin beneath the eyes is so thin, the blood passing through the vessels is easily visible.

The dark circles that appear under our eyes when we are short of sleep are literally pools of blood. Small wonder that "eye brightening" or blepharoplasty – the removal of excess fat, skin and muscle from saggy, baggy upper and lower eyelids – has become the most popular form of cosmetic surgery for men.

why can't we tickle ourselves?

This is a question that has, well, tickled the fancy of many people over the years. Even Charles Darwin tried his hand at solving the puzzle. He concluded that we can't tickle ourselves because we don't find ourselves frightening (well, most of us don't).

According to Darwin, the wriggling and squirming we perform when tickled is part of a natural reflex that helps us escape from attackers when they've grabbed vulnerable parts of our body.

The reason we laugh is because we know the attack isn't real – and we're making this clear to our "assailant". When we're really being attacked, we still wriggle, but don't laugh.

why do we rub our eyes when we are tired?

Because when we are tired, we don't produce enough of the moisture our eyes need, and rubbing them stimulates the tear glands. If your eyes feel dry and itchy several times a day you might have dry eye syndrome. This may be down to not producing enough tears, the mixture of fluids in the eye being unbalanced, or to your tears evaporating too quickly.

Some people naturally produce more tears than others, and those with lower tear production are more likely to have eye irritations. Persistent dryness may be caused by a thyroid condition called Hashimoto's disease, or a glandular disease called Sjogren's syndrome.

why is it hard to say "red lorry, yellow lorry"?

Because your brain gets confused (not your tongue). To prove this, try to mentally articulate "red lorry, yellow lorry" three times in rapid succession, without moving your lips. Then do the same with the phrase "red lorry, black car". Your brain will more than likely trip up over the first phrase but not the second. Why the difference? Because the brain has to "plan" each sound in a string of words or syllables before you can say it. When two or more similar sounds occur close together, the brain gets confused in its plan and you stumble when you try to say the phrase.

Some people, however, have no difficulty with these tongue twisters (which should really be called brain-twisters). Language expert Professor Brian Butterworth of University College, London recalls one student who could say "Peggy Babcock" 120 times in one minute; try it if you've nothing better to do.

could you make a living through donating sperm?

Not in Britain, unless your expenses are tiny. The Human Fertilisation and Embryology Authority (HFEA), created in 1990 to regulate fertility treatments, has set a maximum payment of £15 per donation. Men are also limited to two donations per week and no one is allowed to father more than 10 children (to reduce the risk of half-siblings meeting later in life and reproducing). As donor insemination has a success rate of 8 or 9 per cent, the average man will only be able to donate around 100 times. Where donation for research is concerned, only the twice-weekly restriction holds and some men donate regularly for 18 months to two years.

In America, however, there are almost no restrictions on sperm donation and men can charge what they like. Countless websites are plastered with pictures of smiling would-be donors. A typical ad reads: "I am a US Marine and I need to make $1,700 so I will sell my sperm. I am attractive and in great shape. No mental or physical problems and very long-living family." A big problem with the American system is the lack of screening – donors may be infected with HIV or carry dodgy genes, and then the recipient female may get much more than she bargained for.

How much can someone with an average stomach capacity eat in one session, and how much does one person eat in a lifetime?

Relax, you can't actually keep eating until your stomach bursts. Well, not normally, anyway. Once food gets into the stomach, it is mixed with gastric juices and becomes a soupy liquid called chyme. The stomach has elastic walls and can expand as you eat to hold up to seven pints of chyme. What this translates into in terms of a meal depends upon the bulk of what you eat or drink. If you drink three pints of beer before dinner, you're unlikely to be able to eat a hearty three course meal without feeling uncomfortably full.

Your stomach can't burst because of a hormonal interplay between it and the brain. One hormone, gastrin, opens up the pyloric sphincter to let the chyme into the duodenum for further digestion. Another hormone, cholecystokinin, makes you feel full, so under normal conditions you stop eating.

People suffering from bulimia (from the Greek word *buos* meaning "ox" and *limos* meaning "hunger") override this balancing mechanism and may stuff themselves with up to 40,000 calories (the equivalent of around 20 chocolate gateaux, although most bulimics eat a range of food during a binge) in a session.

In a lifetime, you'll eat an average 2,000 to 2,500 calories a day. If you live for 75 years, this is the equivalent of about a quarter of a million slices of bread, thickly spread with butter.

what's the capacity of a human memory measured in gigabytes?

About 50 gigabytes, according to Igor Aleksander, professor of neural systems engineering at Imperial College, London. He arrives at this answer on the basis that we have about 10 billion neurons in our heads, each neuron holding about five bytes. "It seems surprisingly low," he says, "but the brain gets on quite well with that."

All adults have roughly the same capacity, but there are huge differences in what we can do with it. "Brains differ a great deal from each other," says Aleksander, "sometimes through habit and sometimes through wiring."

Whether a human brain can be replicated inside a computer is an altogether more complex question. "In terms of capacity it would not be difficult to do that," Aleksander says. "But making it act like a human brain is another matter entirely. You need a human being to have a human experience – a machine can only have a machine experience."

Do blind people "see" in their dreams?

It seems to depend on when they lost their sight. "I was sighted until the age of nine and I'm almost always fully sighted in my dreams," says the Royal National Institute of the Blind's communications officer, Phil Jenkins. "But if I dream about someone I know but have never seen, I will know they're there, but I can't see them – my partner, for example."

For those born blind the experience is different. "I have a good imagination and my dreams are often very highly atmospheric," says Wayne Chapman, helpline assistant at the RNIB. "I once dreamt that I was by a swimming pool. Kids were jumping in the water; someone was playing a guitar, someone else was reciting poetry. I suppose the dreams are a combination of sounds, experience and imagination."

Everyone dreams, including the blind. During a dream there is random stimulation of the cerebral cortex, including the visual area. This creates illusory-like sights, sounds, smells and so on, which go to build up the dream experience. As the cortex is unimpaired in most blind people, there is no physiological reason why they can't have dreams (many have a problem with the eye, not the brain, although in certain cases of blindness there is damage to the visual cortex).

But blind people do sometimes find it hard to describe their dreams. What they make of the dream depends very much on their visual experience. It is a common myth that blind people cannot see at all. In fact, very few are "black blind". Most see some light and colours – and these will be reflected in their dream experiences. For instance, people with macular degeneration, a condition of the retina which may occur in older people and diabetics, often see "splashes" of colour.

Most blind people's sight degenerates as they get older, so they will interpret their dreams in the light of their sighted memories. In rare cases people have their sight restored after being born blind and have to "learn" how to see – integrating the visual appearance of objects with their earlier touch-related perception. Apparently, such people find recognising and naming objects relatively easy but have trouble judging distances. What they make of their dreams has never been fully studied.

Is there any hope of a cure for Alzheimer's disease?

Recent experiments have revealed the potential of stem cells – which may, in the future, come from therapeutic cloning – for brain repair. As we get older, we tend to lose axons, the fibres that brain cells use to communicate with one another. But a naturally-occurring substance called nerve growth factor (NGF) can make axons grow again.

A study carried out at the University of California School of Medicine, San Diego, injected cells that had been genetically modified to produce NGF into aged monkeys. It's known that monkeys lose 25 per cent of their axons as they age. After the treatment, the monkeys had axon levels similar to those in young monkeys and, in some cases, higher.

The next stage is to try this on people with Alzheimer's, to see if it can reverse the loss of memory and decline in cognitive function. Two patients are already undergoing trials, and the team is looking for other people to participate.

what disease did the elephant man suffer from?

The Elephant Man – whose real name was Joseph Merrick – was rescued from an East End freak show in 1886 by the eminent Victorian physician Sir Frederick Treves. Yet neither Treves nor any of his colleagues could fathom the cause of the terrible growths and bone deformations that had ravaged Merrick's body since early childhood. Their best guess was that he suffered from some rare "congenital disorder".

Later, experts suggested this may have been an extreme variety of neurofibromatosis-1 (NF-1), a genetic condition that would have gone some way to explaining Merrick's symptoms. Then, in 1986, scientists in Canada argued that Merrick was a victim of the extremely rare Proteus syndrome, another congenital tissue-distorting disease first identified in the late 1970s.

However, neither diagnosis fully fits the facts – which has recently prompted a new theory: that Merrick actually suffered from both of these conditions. As well as accounting for most of his symptoms, this would explain why nothing like Merrick's case has been seen since. NF-1 occurs in around 1 in 2,500 births, while Proteus syndrome affects around 1 in 9 million – implying that there should be only one case of combined NF-1/Proteus Syndrome every 22,500 million births. At that rate, it's unlikely that there will be another Elephant Man born for several centuries at least.

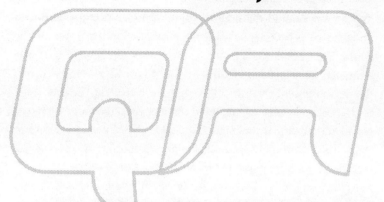

Adventure,
Travel and
exploration

🔵 How do we know the height of Mt Everest?

🔴 It wasn't until the mid-nineteenth century that the mountain now known as Mt Everest was even recognised as the highest in the world. That honour originally went to Kanchenjunga, which was estimated to be 28,000ft (8534m) high (it's now known to be merely the third highest of the world's mountains). In 1852, the British-led Survey of India revealed that there was a peak on the border between Nepal and Tibet that was higher. Called Peak XV, it was stated to be 29,002ft (8,839m) high, an astonishingly accurate figure considering that the peaks were measured from 150 miles away.

In 1865 the mountain was renamed Mt Everest, after a former surveyor-general of India, Sir George Everest. Today's most quoted figure – 29,028ft (8,848m), just 26ft (8 metres) taller than the original figure – is based on measurements made by B. L. Gulatee of India and colleagues during a survey made in Nepal in the early 1950s. This measurement has long been regarded as definitive – even the classic National Geographic 1:50,000 map of the region worked back from this reference height.

But in 1998 an American team led by Wally Berg set off to challenge the accepted reading, using the latest Global Positioning System (GPS) technology to measure the altitude of the highest solid bedrock on the mountain (the actual summit is made of snow, but you add that on later). This rock is called Barry Bishop Ledge (seriously) and it was here that Berg attached the GPS receiver, switched it on and began collecting data. Analysis of that data suggested that the official height of Everest had to be revised downward somewhat.

Precisely how much it should be reduced is still a matter of argument, but according to the team, even taking into account all probable errors, the summit cannot be higher than 8,830m, which is 28,970ft, or about 58ft (18 metres) lower than the textbook value. Nevertheless, as they point out, even with this lower figure, Mt Everest is still the highest mountain in the world by quite a big margin.

🐾 How does the Global Positioning System work?

🐾 The digital age has provided explorers with perhaps the most useful invention since the magnetic compass – the Global Positioning System (GPS), a hand held unit that can tell you where you are in the world to within 10m. Such units are routinely used by adventurers such as David Hempleman-Adams.

Planet Earth is currently orbited by over 20 GPS satellites (this will eventually reach 30), each one broadcasting its own time-signals, created by its own incredibly precise atomic clock. Travelling at the speed of light, these signals are received and compared by the hand-held receiving set, which uses them to calculate exactly where it must be relative to the satellites. There are always at least four GPS satellites above the horizon at all times anywhere on the planet; as a result, the hand-set can calculate longitude, latitude and altitude to within 10m at all times. With a little more effort, that error can be reduced to a centimetre or so.

🐾 If I'm lost without a compass or GPS what should I do?

🐾 Hungarian mathematician George Polya proved in 1921 that anyone who gets lost can eventually get home again by wandering about at random, tossing a coin to decide which way to go next. The trouble is, you may die of old age before the trick works. So it's always a good idea to know which way you're heading. And while GPS handsets and car navigation systems can show where you are anywhere on the planet to within 10m, all technology can go wrong – usually when you really need it. That's when the age-old direction-finding tricks come in handy:

Watch and sun
If you have a (non-digital) watch, you've got a compass. To find out

which way is due south, set your watch to GMT then align it so that the hour-hand points to the sun. Next, imagine a line being drawn exactly between the hour-hand and the "12" marked on the watch dial: that line points due south.

Shadow-stick

If you don't have a watch, you can use the shadow-stick method. Put a stick (around a metre tall) into the ground, and mark the tip of the shadow it casts. Then wait until the shadow has swung around by a few centimetres, and mark the tip of the new shadow: the line joining the two runs east-west.

Polaris: north at night

At night, it's possible to find north by looking for Polaris, the Pole Star. Look for the constellation of the Great Bear (also known as The Plough or The Big Dipper), which resembles a saucepan. Find the two stars forming the side of the pan farthest from the handle, and extend the line they make upwards to the first bright star: that's Polaris.

More moss to south

Nature also provides clues, albeit less reliable. Moss and plants tend to grow on the south side of trees (more exposed to sunlight). Young trees on open ground tend to lean away from the direction of the prevailing wind – which, with Britain's south-westerly wind systems, means they lean towards the north-east.

what was the first place to be digitally mapped?

In 1995 Britain became the first country in the world to be completely digitally mapped, 26 years after starting the process of converting its 230,000 maps.

The resulting "master map", known as the National Topographic

Database (NTD), carries the positions of 200 million features, from mountains and lakes right down to individual telephone boxes and kinks in roadside curbs. Unlike old maps, the NTD is constantly updated, with users such as the utility companies feeding in information on any changes they make.

The Ordnance Survey is currently working on giving every single one of Britain's 40 million buildings its own unique ID code, with information such as its date of construction, its ownership details and its connection to utilities attached.

why do explorers take so long to get to the north pole?

It can take explorers weeks longer to reach the pole than they expect, because of a morale-sapping phenomenon called negative drift. The arctic ice-cap is just a frozen skin of ice floating on top of a three-mile deep ocean. That makes the North Pole itself a moving target for anyone trying to reach it.

In 1997 two British explorers, David Mitchell and Dr Stephen Martin made an unsuccessful attempt to cross the polar ice cap, walking unsupported via the pole from Russia to Canada. For the first 50 days of the expedition the wind blew constantly from the north, which pushed the ice floes back in the direction they had come from. One day they walked for nine-and-half hours, but had actually retreated a mile. On another they woke up to find they'd lost four miles during the night. Getting up each day to find that you've made no progress can test even the most iron will.

The fragile state of the ice also vastly increases the total distance that has to be covered, forcing explorers to dodge round pressure ridges and open water between floes. From where they set out in Russia, Mitchell and Martin faced a direct-line journey of around 580 miles to the North Pole. In the end, the duo had to walk for almost 1,200 miles to reach their first objective, where they decided that enough was enough.

(Q) who is the most travelled man in history?

(A) The world's most travelled man is John D. Clouse from Evansville, Indiana, USA, who has visited all of the sovereign countries and all but two of the non-sovereign countries existing in 1999.

Clouse grew up during the Great Depression of the 1930s. His father, who had been to Europe, told him of its wonders and instilled him with the travel bug.

Clouse saw some of Europe's wonders during World War II, but not under the best circumstances. Becoming a barrister in 1958, he visited Europe for the first time as a tourist. Thereafter, he travelled to a different part of Europe every year.

Discovering the Traveler's Century Club, for those who have visited 100 countries or island groups, he became a member in 1970 and travel mania truly set in. He began to dream of visiting every country and territory in the world. The two destinations still evading him are Bouvey and the Paracel Islands. He has been very close to Bouvey on two occasions, but both times bad weather has prevented him landing.

(Q) How much of the Earth's oceans have been explored?

(A) Less than 1 per cent – and the vast majority of that is around coastal regions. The oceans cover over 70 per cent of the Earth's surface, but only in the last few decades has serious exploration of them begun. The first voyage to explore the depths of the sea was made by HMS *Challenger* in 1872–6. It established that the deep sea was not barren, but full of life-forms such as strange deep-sea fish.

A new wave of ocean exploration began with the Cold War in the 1950s, when the superpowers drew up detailed maps of the ocean depths for their submarine fleets. Echo-sounding revealed that the seabed was just as varied as the visible surface of the

Earth. It also uncovered mountain ranges more than 10,000 miles long and canyons so deep that they could contain Mt Everest. The Mariana Trench in the North-West Pacific, first surveyed in the 1950s, is almost seven miles (11km) deep.

The oceans have sprung many surprises on scientists. In 1979 a French-American submarine discovered what later became known as a "black smoker" – a deep-sea vent spewing water heated to about 350°C by lava below. Around it were previously unknown marine organisms living off the vent's hydrogen sulphide instead of sunlight. This has since led to theories that such vents may have been the birthplace of life on Earth.

🅠 Is it true that dogs were the key to Amundsen conquering the South Pole?

🅐 When Roald Amundsen beat Robert Falcon Scott to the South Pole he took 97 Greenland dogs, whereas Scott chose motorised sleds. And that, according to the Scott Polar Research Institute, was the key to Amundsen's success.

Roald Amundsen and his Norwegian crew set sail on 9 September 1910 and reached the Ross Ice Shelf in a record-breaking four months. He set up winter headquarters in the Bay of Whales using 46 dogs and five sleds to transfer some ten tons of supplies daily to the base camp. He was then able to establish depots quickly and prepare for the long winter.

Then, in early September 1911, the weather cleared, and eight men with sleds pulled by 86 dogs set out for the Pole, 480 miles (772 km) away. "The going was splendid," wrote Amundsen – covering 30 miles (48km) in three days. But on the fourth day they woke to -20°C. The compasses had frozen solid and two dogs froze to death in their sleep.

Amundsen changed the plans. He would lead one group to the Pole, while another explored King Edward VII Land. So, on 20 October, four sleds, each pulled by a team of 13 dogs, set out. They made it to the foot of a range of mountains, which Amundsen named the Queen Maud Range, and the dogs had a feast of seal meat and blubber.

"The dogs are the most important thing for us", he wrote later. "The whole outcome depends on them." So Amundsen made nutrition a priority, and with the disastrous man-eat-dog experiences on the Belgica expedition in 1899 in mind, took a strategic approach this time.

For the final push to the Pole, now 340 miles (547km) away, he took 42 dogs, supplies for 30 days, and began to climb the mountain. After four days, they reached the summit, having carried a ton of supplies to an altitude of 10,000ft. (3,048m). At this point Amundsen shot 24 dogs, as they were no longer needed. He had six more shot to feed the remaining 12 on the trip back. The group stayed at the "Butcher's Shop", as it became known, for a few days before heading off into a raging blizzard.

For the next ten days five men and 18 dogs fought driving snow, 35mph (56km/hr) winds and dense fog, before reaching Devil's Ballroom glacier – the last obstacle.

The men were frostbitten and the dogs exhausted, but they pushed on. At 3pm Friday 14 Dec 1911, the sled meters registered the geographical South Pole. The Norwegian flag was planted, and the team celebrated that night with a meal of seal meat. Scott arrived at the site of the Pole 35 days later (see p78).

should tourists attempt to climb mt Kilimanjaro?

At 19,340ft (5,895m), Kilimanjaro is nearly 10,000ft lower than Everest and relatively accessible, which makes it the mountain everyone thinks they can climb. According to Steve Bell, Managing Director of travel company Jagged Globe, if you're capable of doing a fairly brisk ten miles in the British hills, then you should be able to climb Kili (as it's affectionately known).

But even if you're as fit as a Royal Marine, you should still know the risks. Altitude sickness kills several people on Kilimanjaro every year, says Bell, and people hoping to climb it should first get properly acclimatized. So steer clear of any travel agent that offers a four-day sprint up the mountain tacked onto the end of a safari, says Bell. The majority of people doing this end up too sick to make it to the top.

Bell estimates that acclimatization will require at least two days (his own company offers a climb of the nearby and lower Mount Meru first to get the body primed). Six days should be the minimum for getting to the top, but if you've got more time, take it. Plenty of people get to the summit, but feel so lousy that they don't enjoy the experience.

what's the toughest round-the-world race?

The notorious Vendee Globe, created by French yachtsman Philippe Jeantot, is widely regarded as the most difficult round-the-world challenge. The aim is to sail single-handed, non-stop and unaided around the world from west to east, and it exacts a heavy toll. Since the first race in 1989/90 – where barely half of the 13 starters actually finished – there have been several deaths and many shipwrecks.

In 1996/7 only six of the 16 yachts finished the race, with Christophe Auguin first across the winning line in 105 days. One massive storm in the southern ocean caused three yachts to capsize. Another yacht was later caught in a storm farther east and never seen again.

Only two Britons have ever finished the Vendee Globe – one of them being 24-year-old Ellen MacArthur of England, who came in second in the 2000/01 race, making her both the youngest and fastest woman ever to sail around the world.

what are the effects of high-altitude mountaineering on climbers?

The most serious medical problems encountered by high-altitude mountaineers are caused by lack of oxygen. Oxygen starvation occurs because atmospheric pressure decreases with altitude, so there are fewer oxygen molecules per given volume of air.

At sea level, blood is normally saturated with oxygen. Above 3,000 metres oxygen concentration starts to fall; mountaineers have to acclimatize before going much higher. Normal people lose consciousness when the oxygen level in their blood falls below 55 per cent, but for high-altitude climbers not using supplementary oxygen, concentrations fall well below this.

The mildest form of altitude disorder is known as acute mountain sickness. It's unpleasant but not dangerous in itself. Symptoms are headaches, loss of appetite, nausea and difficulty in sleeping. Vision is also often affected. Almost all Himalayan climbers suffer from it, often on the approach to base camp before they get very high on the mountain.

The real danger with acute mountain sickness is that it can sometimes develop into pulmonary oedema or cerebral oedema – caused by fluid retention in the lungs and brain respectively. The symptoms of pulmonary oedema are breathlessness, coughing (often with blood) and bubbling sounds in the chest. Cerebral oedema is signalled by acute headaches and loss of co-ordination. In both, death follows within a few hours if left untreated. The only effective cure is oxygen – best gained by losing altitude rapidly.

what is the third man syndrome?

Among climbers at extreme altitudes, the lack of oxygen can cause the brain to create bizarre but very realistic hallucinations. For example, when Chris Bonington was nearing the top of Everest in

1985, he saw his climbing partner Doug Scott urging him on – along with his own father-in-law and another unknown man. On his own ascent in 1975, Doug Scott remembers an out-of-body experience with his mind detaching itself from his body and looking down on him from over his left shoulder, urging his legs to keep going.

The so-called Third Man Syndrome – where climbers report an unknown presence at their side – is remarkably common. In 1936, Frank Smythe broke a block of chocolate in half to share with his imaginary climbing friend.

what happens to your body when you go diving without scuba equipment?

If you are diving in cold water, your heart rate slows – a phenomenon known as the "mammalian diving reflex". Simply immersing your face in cold water is enough to make your heart rate decline rapidly. Compression of the chest, as happens at depth due to increased pressure, has the same effect.

The spleens of divers also shrink by up to 20 per cent, releasing extra haemoglobin. All these reflexes go to make divers, such as spear fisherman, more efficient in consuming oxygen.

But pressure is the biggest killer of freedivers, or rather, changes in it. So-called "shallow-water blackout" can occur, due to the compression of the divers' lungs at depth, and subsequent re-expansion while surfacing.

Then there's oxygen starvation. When divers ascend, the lungs re-expand, leaving less oxygenated blood available to the already depleted levels in the body, and the lungs start to suck blood cells back into them from around the body, so more blood is flowing into them than out. This leaves less oxygen available to the brain.

If the diver has been down a long time or performed strenuous exercise at depth, such as fighting a fish, there is a strong possibility he may blackout rapidly at 3-5m – his brain will simply switch off because it's been starved – and if he's not rescued he will drown.

adventure, travel and exploration

where's the best caving to be found in the UK?

In Wales, which boasts the twentieth-longest cave complex in the world (25 miles). At over 1000ft below ground, it is also Britain's deepest system and is known as Ogof Ffynnon Ddu. Oddly, the name means "below the cave", because two brothers, Ashwell and Jeff Morgan, discovered the complex behind a more accessible cave. One of Ogof Ffynnon Ddu's most spectacular features is The Columns – more than a dozen pillars of pure white calcite linking the floor and ceiling. These were precious enough for the complex to be declared Britain's first underground nature reserve.

Elsewhere in Wales, is the spectacular Dan-yr-Ogof complex, which features the stunning "Frozen Waterfall" (a cascade of flowstone), the "Belfry" – with stalactite "ropes" hanging from bell-like boulders – and evidence of a coral colony, a reminder that the cold rock was formed at the bottom of a warm tropical sea more than 300 million years ago.

what should you do if you meet a grizzly bear?

Most bears will try to avoid human contact and most attacks on humans are a case of mistaken identity. Bears are attracted by food smells, so campers in the Canadian bush should keep food (even toothpaste) in a bag suspended from a tree so that it is way beyond the reach of the inquisitive grizzly. But if you do bump into one, don't even think about running away: as soon as you move they will chase you and, while they look fat and slothful, they can run at up to 35 mph.

Instead, if there's more than one of you (and you shouldn't go into bear country alone), cluster together to appear like one big object, rather than two puny ones. Then try and back away. If the bear charges, throw something down like a hat or part of your pack – it may hold his curiosity for long enough for you to escape. If it's too late for that, then play dead, lying face down on the ground with your hands and arms locked over your head. With any luck the bear will then just leave you alone.

what exactly is frostbite?

When exposed to bitterly cold conditions, living tissue on toes and fingers can fall to around minus 5 ℃, at which point it freezes. Water inside the cells turns to ice, which takes up more volume than the original water. Just like frozen pipes in winter, the cells then proceed to burst.

The freezing process in the cells allows a whole variety of other problems to set in, including biochemical changes, dehydration and lack of oxygen. If left untreated, the amount of cellular damage reaches the stage where gangrene takes over – and amputation becomes the only option. Current medical opinion to deal with frostbite recommends rapid thawing in warm water baths.

was sherpa Tenzing Norgay the first man on top of Everest?

It's widely believed that – despite what the history books say – Sherpa Tenzing beat Sir Edmund Hillary to the top of Everest. This rumour continues to circulate in Nepal and India, where the authorities have been keen to claim that it was a Nepalese sherpa that conquered the mountain.

In an interview with *Focus* magazine, Sir Edmund remained adamant the rumours were nonsense. He said: "I led all the way along the Southern Ridge, cutting steps, and then up towards the summit. Then we could see the summit ahead of us. We took in a bit of the rope, and I moved up on top, and I guess Tenzing would have been five or six paces behind." According to Sir Edmund, he and Tenzing agreed to say that they reached the summit "almost together."

But what does Tenzing say? In his 1955 autobiography *Tiger of the Snows*, he recalls the moment: "A little way below the summit, Hillary and I stopped... I was not thinking of 'first' or 'second'; I did not say to myself 'there is a golden apple up there. I will push Hillary aside and run for it.' We went on slowly, steadily. And then we were there. Hillary stepped on top first. And I stepped on after him. The dream had come true."

After climbing Everest Tenzing, the second man to reach the summit, lived in relative obscurity, teaching climbing at the Himalayan Mountaineering Institute in Darjeeling, India. He died in May 1986, aged 72.

How do I avoid jet lag?

Jet lag is an ever-present problem with long distance travel across time zones. You arrive at your destination completely out of sync with local time, and often feel sleepy through the day and wide awake at night.

The body's functions naturally vary in a regular way over time, according to the circadian ("about the day") rhythm. Our body temperature and hormones fluctuate predictably within this cycle. This rhythm is set by our exposure to light and darkness, and determines when we feel sleepy and wide awake.

When we fly long distances we may land in a destination where the sun is rising – even though the place that we left several hours earlier may also have just been getting light or dark. Our circadian rhythm may take a few days to adjust to the "new" timing of day and night and, as a consequence, we suffer from the symptoms of jet lag.

Disturbance to sleep patterns can, however, be reduced if travellers get a dose of the human hormone melatonin – normally secreted at night by the pineal gland – at the right time, rather than at what the body thinks is the right time. Melatonin is thought to help the circadian rhythm adjust more quickly. In trials, volunteers said it made them feel better.

If you are already suffering from jet lag, protein-rich meals taken early in the day can perk you up by providing tyrosine – an amino acid used for producing adrenaline and noradrenaline, which increase alertness. Similarly, the theory goes, carbohydrate meals in the evening will provide tryptophan – an amino acid used for serotonin production, which helps you sleep.

General tips to try during and after long-haul flights include:

1. Start with a good night's sleep before leaving home. Then stimulate your circulation before you set off with a quick jog, brisk walk or some vigorous scrubbing in the shower.
2. Wear loose-fitting natural fibre clothes to allow skin to breathe.
3. Avoid rich or fatty foods the day before travelling, and stick to light meals on board. Steer clear of alcohol, tea and coffee during the flight.
4. Gently performing stretching and breathing exercises in your seat prevents sluggishness.
5. Listen to relaxation tapes, which help you release tension.
6. Use face sprays, lip balm and eye compresses to counteract the effects of dry cabin air.
7. If you're staying abroad for less than 48 hours, don't try to adapt to the new time zone. As far as possible, eat, work, rest and sleep according to your home time.
8. If you're staying for a longer period and need to adjust, expose yourself to natural light.
9. Take a relaxing soak in a bath or a hot shower to help you unwind from the effects of the journey.

🅠 Is there any way of escaping from a sunken submarine?

🅐 Yes, if it's not too deep. As long as it's no further down than around 100ft, then submariners can escape via so-called free ascent, with just a nose-clip. It's more difficult and dangerous than it sounds: there's 3 atmospheres of pressure at these depths – that's 44lbs per square inch – which really hurts the ear-drums. And if you don't release your breath in just the right way, you can suffer severe lung damage – or run out of air before you reach the surface.

Below 100ft, special technology is needed. The Royal Navy has developed an escape suit called the Beaufort SEIS Mark, which can be used to escape from depths of up to 600ft. Below that, specialist rescue vehicles are available, which can clamp on to escape hatches and perform rescues down to 2,275ft. There's no point even thinking about rescue below this, as anything deeper is beyond the crush depth of submarines, at which point the hull finally gives in under the many tens of atmospheres of pressure, and cracks.

🅠 How can I achieve the ultimate "rush"?

🅐 By joining the notorious Dangerous Sports Club, founded in Oxford by David Kirke. He made the Club world-famous on April Fool's Day 1979, by performing the world's first bungee jump. Wearing full morning dress with a grey top hat, and clutching a bottle of champagne, Kirke leapt from the 74-metre-high Clifton Suspension bridge in Bristol and was promptly arrested.

In the late 1970s and early 1980s the antics of the Dangerous Sports Club were rarely out of the news. Its 35 members, described as "quintessential English eccentrics", epitomised the danger-seeking personality. Mostly students from Oxford University, they spent their time devising madcap ways of risking their lives. The club's symbol was a wheelchair with a blood-red seat.

The Dangerous Sports Club was launched with a champagne breakfast on Rockall, a 19-metre-high stack 320 kilometres off the coast of Scotland. Guests were expected to leave the party by jumping into the sea. They once also dined on the rim of the Soufriere volcano on the island of St Vincent in the Caribbean – while it erupted.

In the early 1980s members of the club travelled to St Moritz, Switzerland, to demonstrate alternative skiing techniques. Two formally dressed members slid down an expert run at 40mph, while sitting at a grand piano and playing Mozart. A wooden horse, a bathtub and an inflatable elephant were also all attached to skis and ridden downhill.

The club once built an inflatable melon, five stories high and containing five tons of air. A gimble mechanism (for keeping the contraption upright) allowed them to steer from within. But this didn't prevent the melon from bouncing out of the river it was travelling down and crashing into an electricity pylon, blacking out the whole of Telford.

In October 1992 the club set up as a commercial operation and opened its doors to casual thrill-seekers as well as what it calls "genuine hard-heads looking for the adrenaline fix". Initiation is a bungee jump, and members are kept informed of club activities. See www.btinternet.com/~dafyddk/dsc.htm

which is tougher: Arctic or Antarctic exploration?

Our greatest living explorer, Sir Ranulph Fiennes, was the first to reach both the North and South Poles on foot. And according to him, they're both awful, but in different ways. The wind and cold is more of a problem in the Southern continent, while near the North Pole the ice is always breaking up, and can take you many miles away from your destination.

Q. *who made the first hot-air balloon attempt on the North Pole?*

A. On 11 July, 1897 Swedish scientist Saloman Andreé told onlookers: "Don't be uneasy if you receive no news from me for a year, and possibly not until the following year." And with that he took off from the beach of Danes Island, Spitzbergen, in an audacious attempt to reach the North Pole by hot air balloon. Joining him in the open wicker basket of his balloon, *Ornen*, were two other Swedish adventurers, Knut Fraenkel and Nils Strindberg. The three men were never seen alive again.

The expedition caught the imagination of the world at a time when Sweden and Norway were racing to be the first to the Pole. King Oscar II of Sweden and dynamite inventor Alfred Nobel contributed generously to the cost of Andreé's quest. On Danes Island he built a huge hangar 60m high to protect the balloon from the Arctic winds while it was being inflated. The basket was equipped with a huge amount of kit, much of which betrayed the explorers' ignorance of the Arctic. Along with food rations, a collapsible boat, snow sleds and rifles, were 57lb (26kg) of chocolate cake, 32 carrier pigeons, goose-liver paté and dinner jackets in case the three explorers should meet the monarch of an unknown polar kingdom.

Andreé did not have much luck with his pigeons. One of the first to be released was shot by the captain of a Norwegian sealing vessel, *Alken*, when the bird landed on the ship's rigging. Incredibly, the dead bird was retrieved later that day when *Alken* made a rendezvous with another ship and the captain then learned about Andreé's balloon flight. The message tied to the dead bird's leg was dated July 13, gave the balloon's position and read: "Good speed to E, 10 degrees south. All well on board. This is the third pigeon post. Andreé."

Over 30 years elapsed before the missing men were found. In 1930 a group of hunters on White Island, another corner of Spitzbergen's frozen archipelago, stumbled across a small boat prodruding from a snow bank. Inside the boat were food stores, diaries, sledges, logbooks and rolls of exposed film. The body of Strindberg was buried under a few rocks. The skeletons of Andreé and Fraenkel lay in their sleeping bags under the frayed remains of a tent.

The diaries revealed that *Ornen*'s flight had lasted just three days, crashing on the ice 216 miles (348km) from the nearest land. The balloon had been weighed down by freezing fog – a coating of ice on the envelope – and its trouble further compounded by a gas leak. Somehow, the aeronauts, who had no prior experience of living in the Arctic, had survived for over three months.

The men may have eventually died from hypothermia, scurvy, or trichinosis from poorly cooked bear meat. But what became of the *Ornen*? Its envelope of Chinese silk was used for the men's makeshift tent. Aptly, the balloon that had been the vehicle for Andreé's inflated ambitions in life also provided his shroud in death.

David Hempleman-Adams became the first man to acheive the North Pole in a hot air balloon on 28 May 2000.

what was the largest ever formation skydive?

Would you spend 20 minutes free-falling towards the earth just to hold hands with 295 mates? This extraordinary feat was captured on film in 1996 during a successful bid to break the "largest formation skydive" world record. It smashed the existing 200-skydiver record set in Florida six years ago.

The record breakers threw themselves out of helicopters 20,000ft above the Russian Black Sea resort of Anapa. To give themselves the best chance of success they waited until they reached a height of 6,000ft before pulling the ripcords – even so, it took eight attempts and the full 296-strong link up still lasted for only three seconds. Judges watched a video shot during the jump to verify the attempt. There's no theoretical limit to the number of skydivers who can link up, but it's tricky finding enough aircraft to lift 200-plus bodies to 20,000ft.

Incidentally, during the 1970s, a NASA scientist claimed that 180 linked skydivers would create sufficient drag to make it possible for them to land safely without parachutes. Odd that nobody's tested his theory.

Is it true that scott missed the south pole?

Everyone knows the tragic story of how Captain Scott and his companions were beaten to the South Pole in 1912 by the Norwegian Roald Amundsen. What isn't so well known is that through his own cartographic bungling, Scott and his team never actually got to the South Pole at all.

Like so much else about his expedition, Scott took a "Gentleman–amateur" attitude towards the key issue of navigating his team to the Pole. He originally intended setting out without any qualified navigators, but at the last moment invited Petty Officer Henry Bowers to join the team.

Despite knowing that navigation rules change near to the poles because of "bunching" of lines of longitude, Scott stuck to the conventional methods. This involved Bowers making tricky sightings of the stars using a theodolite, followed by long, complex calculations, all in atrocious conditions.

In contrast, the ever-professional Amundsen took four fully-qualified navigators, a simple sun-sighting sextant and specially simplified calculations to rapidly pin-point his position. The outcome was inevitable. On 18 December 1911, Amundsen reached the Pole and ensured his team actually walked over it. A month later, the exhausted Scott arrived with his team, found Amundsen's tent – and planted a Union Jack at what they thought was the Pole. But due to a blunder in their complex calculations, Scott and his team were actually not where they thought they were. Later analysis revealed that Scott and his companions actually missed the Pole by half a mile.

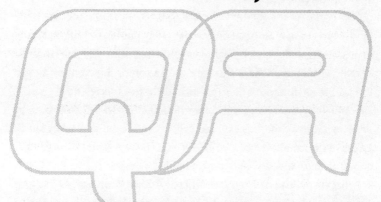

animal magic

animal magic

🔵 Is it possible to determine the sex of a dinosaur?

🔴 Peter Larson, a palaeontologist from the Black Hills Institute of Geological Research, believes so – at least in the case of *Tyrannosaurus rex*, where the clue to the sex of the creature lies in the tailbones. In the smaller individuals of the species, says Larson, the first chevron (one of the spines attached to the tail bone) can be seen to be near the base of the tail, whereas the first chevron of larger individuals (which he believes to be the females) is further down and smaller so as to aid the laying of eggs.

Angela Milner of The Natural History Museum agrees that this is a possibility, but points out it is so far not proven. She adds that even in duck-billed dinosaurs, where one sex boasts a crest or head decoration and the other doesn't, it is still not possible to decipher which is which.

🔵 Why are there so few insects in the sea?

🔴 Of the 1.3 million classified species of insect, only a few dozen have managed to make permanent homes in the sea. All of these species are small, and many are rare and confined to micro-habitats such as algae mats, driftwood or shorelines. There is no evidence from the fossil record that marine insects were any more common in the past.

Given the insects' unmatched diversity, and boldness in colonising other habitats from deserts to freshwater, this reluctance to go to sea seems puzzling.

The most likely explanation, according to biologist J C H van der Hage of Utrecht University, has little to do with fear, but a lot to do with evolution on land. Most modern insects evolved after and then alongside flowering plants, and their survival depends on them. As there are no flowering plants in the sea, it follows that there's a dearth of insects.

Does a book or database exist that classifies every living organism?

Despite centuries of effort, scientists are still far from completing the catalogue of all living things. Says Dr Sandy Knapp, a taxonomist (or classifier) at The Natural History Museum: "We don't even know how many animals there are."

The classification of living organisms on scientific principles began with Linnaeus' *Systema naturae* in 1757, which listed all the animals known at the time. His basic principles and double-barrelled system of names are still the basis of taxonomy today. But the idea of classifying everything has long been abandoned. "There could easily be more than 30 million species on Earth," says Dr Knapp. "By the time we'd got them all classified, there'd probably be an 'E' for extinct by every one."

There is also an important distinction between a classification and a list. A classification is a hypothesis – a suggestion of how species might be related. Classifications tend to be of small chunks of biodiversity – the great apes, say. Lists paint a broader picture, like the 100,000-plus known species of ant, or the flora of Central America. Taxonomists compile both – both have a variety of practical uses, like helping to guide breeding programmes for disease-resistant strains. But it is unlikely that the two will ever be combined into one giant super-classification of every living thing.

Can you get "high" by licking toads?

Most hallucinogenic drugs are manmade – including chemicals like DMT, Ecstasy and LSD – but there are natural psychedelics too. As well as *Stropharia cubensis* (a.k.a. the "magic mushroom", which synthesises a potent drug, psylocybin), psychedelic chemicals are present in the seeds of the morning glory flower, the fungal parasite ergot (the cause of St Vitus' Dance) and the Turkestan mint plant *Lagochilus inebrians*. At least two species of cactus also harbour psychedelic chemicals.

There are psychoactive drugs of animal origin. Some Californians and Australians enjoy licking *Bufo* toads to get a brief psychedelic high, and ancient peoples of the middle Americas used the venom of the Sonoran desert toad as a ritual intoxicant. Though toxic when ingested, it could be safely smoked to get powerful hallucinations from its active ingredient, 5-methyoxy-N,N-dimethyltryptamine.

A similar, though rather more complex, chemical is still used by the Matses Indians of northern Peru. "Sapo" is their name for the skin secretions of the *Phyllomedusa bicolor* which, when rubbed into burned parts of their skin, gives them the impression of increased physical strength, resistance to hunger and thirst and heightened senses.

Are dolphins as cute as we think they are?

Dolphins have a real softie image. But is it justified? Well, yes and no. Dolphins have intelligence comparable to that of a rat, and of the 26 species of dolphin, some have a strong affinity for humans. This has given rise to many stories of dolphins rescuing humans. For example, in 1996 American Martin Richardson was in the Red Sea when he was attacked by a shark. A diving instructor went to his rescue – and found that three dolphins were swimming around Martin and slapping their fins and tail flukes on the water surface, keeping the shark at bay.

Scientists think such rescues simply demonstrate the strong so-called epimeletic instincts of dolphins – their urge to ensure the survival of their species by helping one another: anything about the same size as a dolphin can find itself being rescued. They're not always very discriminating about who or what they rescue, though: dolphins have been known to kill sharks, and then immediately attempt to rescue the carcass by pushing their snouts under it to prevent it from sinking.

Nor are dolphins always as amiable as they might appear: they are hunters and they can defend themselves. Male bottlenosed dolphins – the Flipper variety – are aggressive. The males fight and jostle with each other to gain dominance. Several males will bully a female into mating – if she still resists they will rape her. Adult dolphins can fend off a shark by butting it with their beak, often ramming the shark near its vent – well away from the head. Several dolphins working together can pulverise a shark's internal organs, enough to deter and even kill it.

Dolphins have also attacked humans. Mike Heithaus, a dolphin researcher at Shark Bay in Australia, says: "Handled the wrong way, dolphins bite. They have an array of teeth that can strip the skin from your arm and a tail that can knock you out." Dolphins don't like being touched. A well-intentioned grasp can be mistaken for a biting mouth, in which case the dolphin may respond with a teeth-rake, a tail slap, or, at worst, a head butt. The first dolphin death happened in Brazil in 1994. The dolphin responsible appeared off Sao Paulo and began to socialise with bathers. As he became an attraction, he was surrounded by as many as 30 tourists at a time, and responded by butting a number of bathers, killing one man.

How do birds sit on power lines without getting killed?

Sitting on a power line that is carrying up to 400,000 volts would seem to be a sure-fire recipe for disaster. The reason birds can do it without getting electrocuted is that a bird sitting on a cable isn't in the contact with the ground: it's touching only the cable, and so has the same voltage as the cable. No voltage difference means no electric current, and no current means no electric shock. If, however, the bird flaps its wings and touches another cable at a different voltage – kaboom! Which is why the cables are spaced sufficiently far apart for birds not to get electrocuted.

animal magic

🔵 what's the world's most powerful animal poison?

🔴 The Australian blue-ringed octopus may be small, but it produces the deadliest venom around. Just a few tiny drops can kill a man in minutes. The 15cm-long octopus uses its beak to puncture the skin of its prey, then it floods the area with the venomous cocktail, which it releases through modified salivary glands. The venom targets the respiratory system, stopping the nerve cells functioning, paralysing the area and asphyxiating the victim. As yet, no one has been able to develop an antidote.

While it's pretty hard to come into contact with this venom, Japanese businessmen actually pride themselves on eating seafood that contains a poison hardly less dangerous. Known as tetrodotoxin, it is thousands of times more deadly than cyanide, and is found in the tissue of pufferfish. Made into soup costing over £100 a bowl, it adds a frisson to dining out after a hard week. For if the chef makes a mistake, death could follow before the diner has time to order up the bill and coffee.

🔵 what's the fastest-breeding mammal on the planet?

🔴 When it comes to producing offspring, the female meadow vole is the Ferrari of the animal kingdom. From a standing start at the age of 25 days she can produce litters of up to eight young about 17 times a year. However, she's left at the traffic lights by the insect community. A single cabbage aphid, for instance, could have a mass of descendants weighing 800 million tonnes (over twice the weight of the world's human population) by the end of the year (including all of its children, grandchildren, great-grandchildren etc). Bacteria are equally speedy breeders. The coliform family reproduce every 15 minutes.

How do worm-charmers get worms from the ground?

The traditional method is called "twanging", where a fork is placed in the ground and wiggled. Apparently, the worms find these vibrations irresistible because they mistake them for a rain shower. Worms are drawn to the surface when it rains to avoid their waterlogged burrows.

Can you really have a fish out of water?

Absolutely, the world is swimming with them. The African lungfish not only breathes air, but burrows as well. During the dry season it makes a hole in the dried-up river bed, slithers into it and stays there, happily breathing in fresh air for months at a time.

Mudskippers in fact spend most of their time out of water, using their fins to propel themselves across the ground. But these fish aren't quite what they seem. "They're a bit of a cheat, really," says Jamie Oliver, a marine biologist at the London Aquarium, "because they swallow a huge mouthful of water before they go, which they then pass over their gills." According to the *Guinness Book of Records*, the most reluctant fish is the catfish *Phreatobius walkeri*, which is such a landlubber that if it's put into water it jumps straight back out again.

Can any animals survive without their heads?

Beheaded cockroaches not only survive, they go on living for seven days. There are ways to make them live even longer. In one experiment the head was removed from one cockroach and the legs from another. The legless cockroach was then placed on top of the headless one and the bodies were pierced and "joined" – if the bodily fluids are allowed to mix, the headless cockroach apparently navigates using sensory information from the legless one.

animal magic

But what about those animals that are formed without heads? In October 1997, scientists at the University of Bath revealed that they had used genetic engineering in order to grow headless frogs. No one is sure exactly how long the headless frogs could live for, since they were all killed after three days. But with artificial feeding, there is no biological reason to think that they couldn't survive for longer.

As for humans, there have long been stories about the eyes of beheaded people surveying the crowd as their heads are held up for inspection by their executioner. Pure nonsense, you might think. Yet, according to a study by Dr Harold Hillman of Surrey University, there may well be enough oxygenated blood still in the brain following execution to allow consciousness – and pain – to persist for many seconds.

with advances in genetic engineering, will there ever be a pig that can fly?

It's true that scientists have achieved some pretty impressive – not to say grotesque – achievements over recent years, ranging from genetically engineered fruit flies with legs where their eyes should be to mice with human ears growing out of their back. There are also many examples of single-gene transfers between animals. For instance, there are genetically engineered sheep that can produce a human protein called alpha-1-antitrypsin (AAT) in their milk. AAT is used as a treatment for severe lung disease. The sheep have just one human gene, though, and don't look remotely human.

Even so, it is certainly possible to make bizarre animals by genetic engineering. How about mice with ears that glow in the dark? Transferring the gene for luciferase – the chemical that makes glow-worms glow – to mice in such a way that it switches on only in the ear (or nose or whiskers for that matter) would be relatively simple.

Making a flying pig is an entirely different matter, however. First, no one knows how many genes might be involved in the development of wings and in flying, but there are bound to be many different ones. And the transfer of many interacting genes – rather than just one – between species is currently beyond the scope of genetic engineering. The second problem with flying pigs is that, even if you could breed a pig with flapping wings and aerobatic instincts, its other piggy characteristics – such as weight and body shape – would prevent it from getting off the ground. Given the speed at which the gene scene is advancing, though, it may be better never to say "never".

How do spiders spin webs – and how come they don't get caught in them?

It is thought that there are around 100,000 species of spider worldwide, some of which don't even construct a web, while others produce only tangles of thread. But around one species in 10 are "orb weavers", creating webs that resemble wheels, with a central hub from which spokes radiate and a spiral mesh circling round the spokes. Dr Samuel Zschokke of the University of Basel in Switzerland has been systematically studying exactly how spiders go about constructing their webs.

He has found that, despite having several eyes, most web-spinning spiders have poor vision, and make their webs using their legs to measure distance and tension. Spiders seem to have a built-in engineering knowledge that they use to construct the radial spokes of their nets in a precise order, so that the tension on the web is equal on all sides and the hub remains central.

The finished web has around 40 metres of thread in it and, while it may look as if it's all made from the same stuff, it isn't. The spider begins by allowing a very fine filament of silk to blow on the wind until it sticks to a suitable object. It then builds a Y-shaped frame of tougher silk, weaving a little central "island" into it, along with a temporary spiral. Using this as a guide, the spider then starts producing a sticky thread around the outer parts of the web. Then it fixes shorter sections of sticky thread closer to the central island. The spider leaves some areas of non-sticky thread, though – giving it access to any fly that is caught in the web, wherever it lands.

How do homing pigeons find their way home?

Homing pigeons have such a fine sense of direction that they're able to trace their owner's loft from up to 1,000 miles away. But no one knows for certain exactly how they do it. Scientists think that the birds use the sun for orientation, but experiments with night-flying pigeons show it's not the only means at their disposal. Some researchers believe pigeons have an in-built compass and use the Earth's magnetic field to find their way home. Other homing instinct theories include orientation by smell or even low frequency sound.

Many top breeders boost their birds' abilities with a complex system of training, drugs and vitamins. James Higgins, of the Northside animal hospital, recommends a total programme to enhance young birds' performances, including pox vaccination and drugs.

What happens to fish when they go over waterfalls?

That all depends on the size of the fish and the ferocity of the waterfall. A small weir wouldn't be a great problem to a fish, but it would be unlikely to survive a plunge over Niagara.

In fact, fish do their best to avoid waterfalls. They'll change direction and swim against the tide to locate a deeper channel of water, avoiding strong currents and being swept over the brink. Powerful fish, such as salmon and trout, are very skilful at this and can even leap back upstream.

🐜 If there was an insect olympics, who would win?

🐜 The weightlifting gold would go to the rhinoceros beetle, which can support up to 850 times its own weight. "There are thousands of rhinoceros beetles – even some small ones in the UK", according to Dr John Maunder of the medical entomologist unit in Cambridge. "But the strongest and largest are the African variety. They have to be strong enough to scrape out large amounts of earth and huge stones to make nests."

In sprinting, cockroaches are invincible. The *Periplaneta americana* cockroach has been clocked at 5.4km/h – which, size for size, is equivalent to Linford Christie running the 100m in just over one second. At this speed, the cockroach actually runs on just its two back legs. "It's an escape mechanism which they can only do for a short time," says Maunder. "Cockroaches are normally found on the floor of the forest where they need to escape rodents and spiders."

The high jump master is the cat flea, which can jump 130 times its own height – an astronomical 34cm, and the equivalent of a human jumping over a 70-storey skyscraper. "There's a rubber-like ball in the hip joint of the back legs," says Maunder. "The flea uses large muscles to compress the ball. A trigger muscle is pulled and the stored energy is whipped out through the legs. This makes all the jumps the same height. "Most insects are badly affected by the cold. This method means that fleas can jump just as efficiently in cold weather as hot."

Jumping this high could be dangerous. The g-force experienced by the flea is 100g – equivalent to a car going from 0 to 60 mph in around 0.03 seconds. "But the flea's outer shell acts as a pressure suit," says Maunder. Just as well.

animal magic

Ⓠ what are the world's most dangerous sharks?

Ⓐ According to the International Shark Attack File's list of killers there are 23 man-eating species, but the great white – which grows to 7m – is the most feared.

The File has recorded 311 great white attacks on humans. The tiger shark, which has been called the "hyena of the seas" for its scavenging habits, has 104 attacks on file. Third in the list is the bull shark with 69 attacks. Like the tiger shark it's not fussy about what it eats and is one of the few sharks that can enter fresh water. The sand tiger (or grey nurse shark) is regarded by most divers as harmless but it is gaining a reputation for attacking spearfishermen (53 attacks).

Other sharks to watch out for include the shortfin mako, or mackerel shark, a popular oceanic game fish (38 attacks); the hammerhead (34 attacks, most of which are attributed to the great hammerhead); the blue shark, which is renowned for attacking survivors of ship-wrecks (30 well-documented attacks, but probably more); and the grey reef shark, known for its territorial display to scare intruders (10 attacks, one fatal, some against divers feeding the sharks fish).

Ⓠ why did the dinosaurs die out?

Ⓐ The most likely theory pins the blame on an asteroid impact 65 million years ago, and was put forward in 1980 by a team led by the American physicist and Nobel Prize winner Luis Alvarez. The impact would have triggered global fires, huge tsunamis and a "nuclear winter", in which the smoke thrown up by the impact and fires blotted out the sun for months, killing off plants. The resulting disruption of the food chain would have caused widespread starvation and death. In the early 1990s a crater was found at Chicxulub on the Yucatan Peninsula of Mexico. With an estimated age of 65 million years, it appears to be the site of the impact.

Many experts believe that it would have taken more than this one disaster to knock the dinosaurs off their evolutionary perch, however: having ruled the planet for over 100 million years, the chances are they had already survived one such impact before. Massive volcanic eruptions over what is now the Deccan Traps of India are also thought to have played a role in the final demise of the dinosaurs.

There is no shortage of other theories. For example, according to the greenhouse gas theory, volcanic eruptions 65 million years ago would have filled the air with carbon dioxide, creating a massive greenhouse effect. The volcanic gases and high temperatures may have caused sterility in some dinosaurs which would have disrupted the food chain. Dr M L Keith, a professor at Pennsylvania State University, also suspects that volcanic gases eroded the upper layers of ozone in the atmosphere. This erosion allowed in more ultraviolet light than they could manage. In other words, they died from skin cancer.

Then there's the thin eggshells theory, according to which stresses such as overcrowding affected the female dinosaurs, who began to produce too much oestrogen, resulting in ever thinner and more vulnerable egg shells.

Strangest of all is the hay-fever theory, which pins the blame on the appearance of flowering plants (angiosperms) in the late Cretaceous period and suggests that the dinosaurs were allergic to them.

I fancy getting a pet crocodile. Are there any reasons why I shouldn't go ahead and get one?

There certainly are. Each year, the saltwater crocodile kills around 2,000 people and its Nile counterpart disposes of around 1,000. The saltwater crocodile is misnamed because it can live just as happily in freshwater; many people are killed because they don't know this fact. It has been found as far as 1,125km inland and 1,000km off the coast.

Crocodilians appeared 200 million years ago. A fossil of an eight-million-year-old alligator in the Amazon shows it was 12m long and weighed 18 tonnes – larger than *Tyrannosaurus rex*. Apart from birds, crocodiles are the closest living relatives of dinosaurs. The largest modern crocodile lived in the Segama river of northern Borneo. A saltwater crocodile, it is thought to have been more than 10m long.

🅠 Are there many homosexual animals?

🅐 Yes, there are. One man has even gone so far as to write a book about them. In his 500-page tome *Biological Exuberance: Animal Homosexuality and Natural Diversity* Bruce Bagemihl describes the varied mating patterns of a huge range of species, from birds and bees to bonobos (pygmy chimpanzees). All have been observed and documented exhibiting homosexual behaviour, including same-sex copulation.

In the case of the bonobos, for which virtually every aspect of life revolves around sex, bisexuality is the norm rather than the exception. A wide variety of sexual activities are frequently recorded taking place between male or female pairs of bonobos. At other times, the same animals will mate with members of the opposite sex. For them, as with humans, copulation seems to be less about the business of reproduction than social bonding between individuals.

Bagemihl, who formerly lectured on cognitive science at the University of British Columbia, Canada, describes not just one-off sexual encounters between animals of the same sex but often long-term relationships. He has gathered together a massive body of evidence from scientific papers and journals that over the years has also documented homosexual courtship patterns, affectionate behaviour, pair-bonding and even same-sex parenting in a variety of species. The fact that his book has been critically acclaimed by almost everyone who has reviewed it, including *BBC Wildlife* and *Time* magazines, suggests that the prejudice towards homosexuality which only exists in our species is based on ignorance. To say "It just isn't natural" is patently untrue.

While sexual relations between male mammals, a type of behaviour indicating dominance, is not that unusual among cattle and dogs, it has only rarely been observed among felines because of their solitary lifestyles. However, lions are an exception, as a pride is an incredibly tight-knit community. Even young males ousted from the pride form strong alliances.

How do insect swarms know where to go?

Bees sit at home and wait for a scouter bee to tell them where to find food. If the scouter bee is successful, she (all worker bees are female) arrives back at the hive buzzing with excitement, and carries out a peculiar wiggle, sting first, which shows the others which direction to go.

Locusts are freer spirits, going where the wind and the scent of food take them. A locust swarm can cover an area 1,000km square and 1,500m high, with around 40 million locusts per cubic kilometre. The swarm can travel 100km a day, eating its own weight in food every 24 hours – around two tons for every million locusts – wreaking untold havoc.

which animals can come back to life?

No animals actually come back to life, but toads have a remarkable capacity for lying dormant for years. Throughout history there have been reports of toads found having survived unharmed entombed inside walls. Because it's pretty easy to check when a building was put up it has become accepted that toads can live holed up for 30 years or more.

In some remote desert regions in Australia where it may not rain for years, frogs still manage to thrive. They sit out the drought hidden in a chamber a metre underground, wrapped in a cocoon of dried mucus.

Both the Catholic and the Flat-headed frog are adapted for this, and when they prepare for dormancy their bladders expand to the point where they can conserve water for roughly seven years. In this condition the frogs look like water-filled balloons, and aborigines have been known to drink from them. The frogs are lured out of dormancy by the sound of the rains hitting the surface of the earth.

when a bee stings it dies. is there an explanation for this defence system?

Most bees are solitary creatures and are unlikely to sting unprovoked. Hive-dwelling bees have a sort of "neighbourhood watch" system and will sting in defence of their nest. Among them, only the honeybee dies after stinging. The female honeybee has a unique barbed sting, which is designed to tear and separate from the abdomen along with the venom sac. Unfortunately, the loss of the sting injures the bee fatally.

This drastic action appears to be a specific defence against vertebrates (animals with backbones). When honeybees attack other insects, their stings remain attached.

A detached sting embeds itself deeper and deeper into the flesh, while pumping venom into the wound. At the same time, the sting produces "alarm pheremones". These are volatile chemicals that alert nearby bees to the intruder's presence and signal them to attack. The main component of the pheremone is isopentyl acetate, which smells like bananas. So, be warned: don't eat bananas near a beehive, or if you do, wear a beekeeper's veil.

Do sperm whales really melt their heads?

In a way, they do. The head of a sperm whale has 500 gallons of spermaceti oil, which changes from solid to liquid with a small shift in temperature. John Harwood of the Sea Mammal research unit at St Andrew's University says "It's been suggested whales switch the state of the oil to alter their buoyancy."

Sperm whales dive to depths of 2,000m and these changes could help them rise or sink more quickly than they could otherwise. But Harwood doesn't think this is very likely: "Consider how long jelly takes to set. Then imagine a 2–3 tonne jelly the size of a whale's head. The "melting-solidifying" process would take too long to be of any use."

How do fish keep their teeth in shape?

Not all fish have teeth but for those that do, grinding them down regularly on coral or rocks is very important. If they fail to do so, their teeth may grow too large. Recently, a fish actually had to visit a dentist to get his teeth fixed. A Chicago puffer fish named Eddie, who had been reluctant to adopt the nibbling habit, was not able to eat because his teeth had grown from one quarter of an inch to three quarters of an inch.

Gently holding Eddie's head out of water, dentist Dr Edmond Hanley used a diamond-edged drill to file down the teeth in gentle, 30-second spells. The reason for this was to subject Eddie to as little pain as possible, as puffer fish inflate to three times their usual size in stressful situations.

His teeth back to normal, Eddie is now back to his diet of shrimp and fish food, and regaining the weight he'd lost. There won't be a problem in getting him future dental appointments: his new home is a tank in Dr Hanley's waiting room.

animal magic

How many sheep are there in Australia?

Australia is home to no fewer than 132 million sheep, which makes it the wool capital of the world. (There are, says the UN, around 1.2 billion sheep on the planet – how they counted them all without nodding off isn't known.) Sheep outnumber Australians by eight to one, a ratio exceeded only in New Zealand where there are 17 sheep for every Kiwi and anyone shouting "mint sauce" is arrested.

Which animals can live without water?

Camels can function perfectly well for up to seven days without having to drink any water at all. However, they don't waste the opportunity when it does become available. They have been known to drink more than 100 litres of the stuff in just 10 minutes – enough to kill other animals of a similar size.

Koalas are also able to survive on little water, which explains why their name is the Aboriginal for "no water". They get most of their liquid from eating eucalyptus leaves but koalas have occasionally been spotted drinking at the edge of streams.

Can I buy a painting by an animal?

For just $250, you'll soon be able to buy yourself a painting by one of the art world's rising stars: a trained Thai elephant. The Russian artists Alex Melamid and Vitaly Komar have opened three elephant painting schools in Thailand: one in Lamphant in the north, one in the central ancient capital of Ayutthaya and one on the island of Phuket. The plan is to sell the paintings in the US and channel the profits back to elephant projects in Thailand via the World Wildlife Fund.

Asian elephant numbers have dropped rapidly in recent years. There are now 3,100 in Thailand, compared with 3,600 just two years ago. Elephant handlers have to spend about $27 a day just on feed. Some give the elephants amphetamines so they can work at logging through the night. Others earn money giving rides to tourists. And some are forced to kill the animals when they can no longer afford to feed them.

Animal art is already a commercial success: chimp paintings can fetch high prices in the West, but, as Melamid says, elephants have a more abstract style. "Elephants are not as smart as humans but I'm not sure you have to be smart to be a great painter," he says. "In fact, some of the greatest painters were dumb." And his defence to critics of the quality of his protégés' work? "The thing is, no one knows what art is."

Do animals have paranormal abilities?

Yes, according to some scientists. At the Odier Foundation in Nantes, Dr René Peoch has been investigating the abilities of animals to demonstrate psychokinesis, the supposed ability of the mind to affect physical objects.

His experiments involve a mechanical robot that moves around according to the dictates of a random number generator. If creatures do have psychokinetic abilities, the theory is that they might be able to affect the randomness of the movement, and compel the robot to do what they want.

In one experiment Dr Peoch put the robot in a hatchery, where it became the first object seen by newborn chicks. They regarded it as their mother, and followed it about in its random wanderings.

After three days, Dr Peoch took all but one of the chicks out – and this time prevented the one remaining chick from chasing its robotic "mother". Analysis revealed that the robot now spent more time close to the chick than before – as if the chick had somehow willed his robotic mother to spend more time with him. When the experiment was repeated with chicks that had never seen the robot before, they failed dismally to affect its movements: it seemed they hadn't "tuned in" to the robot's random number generator.

Dr Peoch then carried out similar tests using rabbits – which, unlike the chicks, find the random movements of the robot terrifying. Sure enough, the robot eventually spent more time on the far side of the cage from the rabbits, as if they had willed it away.

Are there any truly dumb animals?

Perhaps the world's quietest creature is the giraffe; it can't make a sound. Despite their gentle giant appearance, giraffes are definitely in the "look but don't touch" category, as far as the rest of the animal kingdom are concerned.

Standing aloof near the top of the food chain, the giraffe is a laid-back sort of guy. Until he's riled; then he'll deliver a well-aimed kick powerful enough to kill a lion.

What's the fiercest mammal in the world?

According to your very own *Focus*, the world's most dangerous mammal is the hippopotamus. The cartoon hippo is a rotund, docile creature with comical teeth and a pink tutu. The reality is a bad tempered, territorial killer with huge, razor-sharp incisors. Hippos kill hundreds of people every year, in more unprovoked attacks than all the other African big game animals put together.

Bryan Dempster, a crocodile-hunter, was on the Zambezi one night with his assistants when their boat was lifted out of the water. The outboard motor screamed until it was slammed back into the water and broken. The hippo crushed the boat in its teeth and the party was dumped into the river. Dempster stayed as quiet as he could, but one of his assistants, Albaan, couldn't swim, and panicked. Dempster saw the hippo charge, slam its giant jaws over Albaan's upper half and take him under the surface to tear him apart.

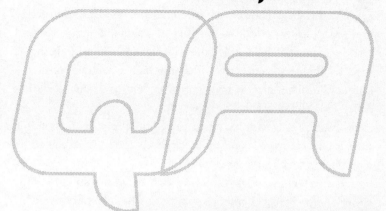

chapter 5

world of science

ⓜ Is there any real rival to diamonds?

ⓐ Artificial diamonds were first made in 1953, but even today they are typically far too small for anything but industrial use. And while compounds like cubic boron nitride come close to being as hard as diamond and can withstand higher temperatures, the uniquely resilient arrangement of carbon atoms in diamonds has never been surpassed for sheer toughness.

Ironically, however, the most prized property of diamonds – their brilliance, sparkle and multicoloured "fire" – is surpassed by a number of far cheaper materials.

Even well-cut lead crystal can surpass the glitter and fire of the cheap and badly cut diamonds sold by some high street jewellers. The problem with lead crystal is that it is basically just glass to which lead oxide has been added – and so is far less hard than diamond. Unless cared for, lead crystal jewellery can end up tarnished and chipped.

In recent years, however, two real rivals to diamond have emerged – both almost as hard as diamond, and both costing a small fraction of the price of the "real thing". The best-known of the two is cubic zirconia – zirconium dioxide – whose refractive index (roughly speaking, the ability to bend light and create sparkle) is almost as good as diamond. More important, however, is the so-called dispersion coefficient of cubic zirconia, that is, its ability to split up and refract light of different colours. This is around 50 per cent greater than that of diamond, giving cubic zirconia substantially more "fire" – and for just a few per cent of the price.

Even more impressive is moissanite, an artificially created diamond substitute whose appearance is so good that when it first arrived on the market in the late 1990s, many jewellers were fooled by it. Unlike cubic zirconia, moissanite's density is almost identical to that of diamond, but both its refractive index and dispersion coefficient are significantly higher.

Jewellers maintain that nothing has the cachet of diamonds, whose amazing properties were forged in the primordial earth countless aeons ago. Well, perhaps – but if you're more interested in having spectacular jewellery than a spectacular overdraft, then nothing beats well-cut moissanite – which costs 10 times less than diamond.

what makes a cricket ball swing?

The sight of a cricket ball visibly swerving in mid-air can be pretty startling, especially as there seems to be nothing near the ball capable of making it move. But there is, of course, the air. On its way to the bat, the ball has air flowing over its surface, and if that flow can be made slightly different on one side, it changes the air pressure, making the ball "swing".

Fast bowlers can create this asymmetry by releasing the ball with its stitched seam at a slight angle, thus triggering turbulent airflow around just one side. Under the laws of cricket, it is also permissible to alter the airflow around the ball by making one side smoother with spit and polish. But it is illegal to make the ball rougher by picking at the leather or the seam. While the basic physics is well understood, the fine details remain mysterious. Exactly why humid air creates more swing, or how bowlers such as Wasim Akram and Darren Gough can create "reverse swing", is still being hotly debated.

Footballers, notably David Beckham, can achieve the same effect by kicking the ball off-centre, thus making it spin about its axis as it travels towards the goal. The air travels faster over the side of the ball moving in the same direction as the spin, and this sets up a so-called Magnus Effect, curving the trajectory of the ball. Again, the effect can be pretty impressive: calculations suggest that it's possible to swerve a football well over 4 metres off its straight-line trajectory – more than half the width of the goal-mouth, and enough to give any keeper pause for thought.

💿 why can't you ever reach the end of a rainbow?

💿 Because there isn't one. Rainbows are circles, or at least, they would be if the horizon didn't get in the way. As a result, rainbows often appear as if they have an end, but this is simply an optical illusion. If you were in an aircraft, you'd be able to see the whole thing – a series of concentric coloured rings, with the shadow of the aircraft in the centre.

The first person to explain the shape of a rainbow was the great seventeenth-century French philosopher and mathematician René Descartes. Using a glass ball filled with water to represent a raindrop, he measured how rays of light from the sun were bent and reflected back toward an observer. This revealed that the rays emerged from each raindrop after having been bent through about 42 degrees (the precise amount depending on the wavelength – and thus colour – of the light). And this explains why we don't see a vertical sheet of colours: we can only see rays from raindrops in such a position in the sky that their 42-degree bending effect sends the rays straight into our eyes. All the rays meeting this requirement lie on a circle, the visible section of which we call a rainbow.

💿 if you drop a ball in a moving car, why doesn't it move towards the back?

💿 It certainly does seem obvious that the ball should move backwards some distance by the time the ball hits the floor. But remember that it's not just the car that is doing, for example, 30mph: it's also everything in the car – including the ball. So, when it's dropped, the ball is still going forwards at 30mph and thus keeps pace with the rest of the vehicle. However, things will change if the car accelerates as the ball falls. Then the ball really will travel backwards – because, once it begins to fall, it has no way of increasing its speed to keep up with the increasing speed of the car.

In fact, if you didn't know that the driver had hit the accelerator, you might even think a force had grabbed the ball and propelled it backwards – which, amazingly enough, is a key idea at the heart of Einstein's theory of gravity, known as general relativity. He recognised that if you drop a ball in a rocket whose engines are accelerating the vehicle upwards, the effect on the ball is the same as if it wasn't moving at all, but gravity was tugging it downward. This in turn led Einstein to a whole new way of thinking about gravity.

The same effect can be turned on its head and used to cancel out gravity, causing weightlessness. If you were in a lift when someone cut the cables and disabled the safety catches, you'd accelerate towards the ground under the effect of gravity. But if you dropped a ball from your hand during your descent, you'd notice that the ball seemed to be motionless relative to you – as if it were weightless. What's happening, of course, is that both you and the ball are freefalling under gravity at the same rate, so it appears as if nothing is happening (until you both smash into the ground).

DO waterfalls freeze?

Yes. According to experts at the Water Research Centre in Marlow, Essex, more or less anything will freeze given the right conditions. A waterfall that contains plenty of rock particles can freeze at just one or two degrees below zero, because the particles act as nuclei around which ice can form.

Waterfalls freeze from the edges inwards, forming stalactites in the process. Huge slabs of ice, between 12 and 24 metres thick, are normal around Niagara Falls during winter. But the main body of water never freezes. That's due to its sheer volume and speed – hundreds of thousands of gallons hurtle down the falls every second – and also to the depth of the pool at the bottom. However, hardy tourists who brave the winter snow can usually see the spectacle of a giant ice bridge which forms at the base of the falls and stretches over part of the river below.

🅠 A friend told me that Mt Everest isn't the highest point on Earth. Is she right?

🅐 Yes – if by "highest" she means the point farthest from the centre of the Earth. Because of the rotation of the Earth, our planet bulges at the Equator, making places in equatorial regions up to 22km farther from the Earth's centre than those at the poles. In the case of Mt Everest, the latest measurement of its height, announced by the US National Geographic Society in 1999, puts the summit at 8,848 metres above sea level. However, at 28 degrees North, the Earth's radius is about 4,700m smaller than it is at the Equator. And that means Mt Everest loses the title of highest point on the planet to Ecuador's Mt Chimborazo, which lies just one degree from the Equator. Though its summit is only 6,267m above sea level, Mt Chimborazo benefits from the bulge in the Earth's shape, so that its summit stands almost 2,100m higher above the centre of the Earth than Mt Everest.

🅠 When is the oil going to run out?

🅐 Probably never, according to Michael Lynch, a political scientist at the Massachusetts Institute of Technology. While the world's wells pump out around 75 million barrels a day (the exact figure depending on how high the oil-producing countries want to drive the price of oil), new fields have been found that could add substantially to those already known. Fields in the Gulf of Mexico, Brazil and Angola could add 75,000 million barrels of oil to the world's reserves, while exploration of the deep field beneath the Caspian Sea suggests this could harbour 200,000 million barrels, making it one of the largest oil basins ever discovered.

And that's all assuming that the world's supplies of oil are fixed. According to Professor Thomas Gold of Cornell University, the standard view of fossil fuels as being the result of geological processes on dead organisms is quite wrong. He has found evidence that coal, oil and gas are all produced by the constant upwelling of carbon-based compounds from deep below the Earth's surface, where they have been trapped since the formation of our planet 4.5 billion years ago.

There's a simple way of testing Gold's claim. According to conventional theory, oil should only be found in regions which 300 million years ago were primordial swamps. According to Gold, however, that's irrelevant: all that's actually necessary is to drill down deep enough into the Earth's surface to reach the places where oil is still being created.

In the 1980s, Gold predicted that oil could be found in the so-called Siljan Ring structure deep in the heart of Sweden – during the late 1980s, engineers succeeded in extracting oil from this very unpromising patch of granite. Many geologists are sceptical of Gold's claim, but there's no denying that he found oil where none was expected. If he really is right, we should also stop worrying about running out of oil; all we have to do is dig deeper.

why don't clouds fall from the sky?

Clouds are comprised of very small water droplets or ice crystals, and sometimes a mixture of both. They are formed when the air is forced to rise, usually because it has become warmer, and less dense, than the air that lies above it. (Alternatively, it might be because the air is following the ascent of a hill or mountain). As the air begins to rise, it cools and eventually reaches what is known as the "condensation level". Once it has cleared this condensation level, the air becomes saturated, and the water vapour that's present starts to condense into water droplets, allowing clouds to develop.

But "if a cloud was to sink back towards the ground, the air would gradually warm, the cloud would pass back through the condensation level, and the water droplets would evaporate – signalling the end of the cloud," says Elizabeth Parr of the British Meteorological (Met) Office.

However, there are situations when it is possible to have clouds at very low levels. As Parr says: "Fog is really only a cloud which is on the surface. The cloud hasn't fallen from anywhere – it's just a case of the condensation level being at a very low height. This means the air becomes saturated very near the ground's surface."

Are there any more chemical elements to discover?

There are only 90 chemical elements which occur naturally, around a third of which appear as separate elements, the rest in combination with other elements. But that hasn't stopped scientists wanting to improve on nature by making artificial chemical elements. Throughout the Cold War, US and Russian scientists competed with each other to find new elements by firing beams of atoms into targets with ever greater force. These so-called transuranic elements (ie "beyond uranium", Element 92) are so unstable that they disintegrate in just a few seconds.

The first transuranic element was neptunium, discovered by the American Ed McMillan in 1940. Then over the next 25 years the field was dominated by Glenn Seaborg of Berkeley University, California, who found new elements ranging from numbers 94 to 102.

The current list stands at 112, which is just two short of the Holy Grail of scientists trying to create new elements: Element 114. Theoretical calculations made in the 1960s showed that this element should be extremely stable, with a lifetime of years rather than fractions of a second. Scientists involved in the hunt for Element 114 reckon that it will take at least to the end of this decade to create it and carry out tests to confirm the beliefs of theoreticians.

However, just because they are esoteric doesn't mean that transuranic elements are useless. Plutonium (Element 94) is notorious for its role as the core of nuclear weapons, while americium (Element 95) is used in fire detectors, to electrically charge the smoke particles and thus trigger the alarm.

🔹 Are there any decent sex scandals in science?

🔹 Many scientists appear to be pretty obsessive types, but some of the most brilliant have given the lie to this strait-laced image.

Einstein had a magnetic effect on women – he had a number of affairs during his two marriages, and once declared: "Marriage is the unsuccessful attempt to make something lasting out of an incident". He divorced from his first wife Mileva (whom he'd married after finding he'd made her pregnant) after starting an affair with his cousin, Elsa. But while the second marriage lasted until Elsa's death, Einstein continued to have various liaisons with women. Their identities, and the intensity of the affairs, are still disputed by historians, but writers Roger Highfield and Paul Carter have found evidence that they involved one of his secretaries, Betty Neumann, a beautiful Austrian blonde named Margarette Lebach, and two wealthy women: Elsa Mendel and Estella Katzenellenbogen. Alice Kahler, the wife of a distinguished German historian, told biographer Denis Brian that she had a photograph of Einstein on which he'd written of his regret that they hadn't slept together.

Not surprisingly, Einstein's roving eye did not go down well with Elsa, causing bitter arguments. It caused similar ructions among those married to the women Einstein took a shine to. The American dramatist Clifford Odets was so incensed by Einstein's ogling of his new wife that he took a pair of scissors to the photos of the meeting and removed Einstein's head.

Erwin Schrödinger, the Austrian physicist and Nobel Prize winner, whose equation lies at the heart of quantum theory, was another notorious womaniser. When he was not beavering away with second-order differential equations, this bespectacled genius was hard at work on his other interest: sex. According to his biographer, Walter Moore, Schrödinger was "devoted to it as the principal non-scientific occupation of his life".

Schrödinger's diaries are packed with accounts of affairs that left a string of women pregnant right across Europe. Escaping from the Nazis – and a few tricky encounters with husbands – in 1933, he turned up at the Institute for Advanced Studies in Dublin to work on a unified theory of the cosmos. And along with him came his wife, his mistress and one of his many illegitimate children – all of whom, he airily informed the authorities, were to be treated as equals. Not that he himself did, of course: once he had his office sorted out, he set about acquiring a few more mistresses.

Rumour has it that Schrödinger made his greatest discoveries in between intensive sex sessions with a woman in an Alpine chalet. Certainly the American physicist Richard Feynman, who won the Nobel Prize in 1965, found inspiration in the naked female form. With three wives and countless lovers, Feynman was a famous habitué of California's topless bars, where he would ogle the girls while solving problems of mind-bending complexity on the beer mats. At least it was cheaper than having affairs with other men's wives – as Feynman knew, from the sums demanded by irate husbands whose wives he had seduced.

Torrid affairs are not the sole preserve of brilliant male scientists, either. On 4 November 1911, Marie Curie found her name plastered across *Le Journal*, one of the biggest-selling papers in France. "A story of love: Madame Curie and Professor Langevin" ran the headline above a report about her affair with physicist Paul Langevin, one of France's most brilliant scientists.

The story, based on outraged testimony from Langevin's mother-in-law, painted Curie as a shameless home-breaker who'd lured a colleague away from his wife and children. Marie issued a strong rebuttal and within 24 hours had received a grovelling apology. Even so, the fact that she was having an affair could not be denied and the newspapers were soon back on the scent. The drama intensified a few days later when Marie was declared winner of the 1911 Nobel prize for Chemistry. But a letter from a committee member all but insisted that she refuse it and stay away from the ceremony. Marie ignored the letter and went anyway. In the end, the furore drove Marie and Langevin apart. She went back to the lab, while he returned to his wife and took a low-profile mistress instead.

what's the best thing to do if you are caught in a lightning storm?

Around a dozen people are killed by lightning each year. If you can't get indoors or into a car quickly, your best bet is to head for low ground as far away from trees and overhead cables as possible, leaving behind any metal objects you're holding – especially umbrellas.

If you start to feel your hair stand on end, you're about to be struck by lightning. In that case, do not lie down: that could lead to the lightning bolt passing through your heart, killing you instantly. Instead, crouch down low putting your hands on your knees. That should ensure the bolt goes through your arms rather than your heart – and that you live to tell the tale.

why is July the hottest month when we're most distant from the sun?

The Earth is indeed about five million kilometres further away from the sun in July than it is in January. But while that might sound a lot, it's just a few per cent of the radius of the Earth's orbit, and has only a minor effect on the amount of heat we get from the sun. Much more important is the effect of the Earth's tilt.

During the summer months, the northern hemisphere is tilted towards the sun, so its rays strike the Earth less obliquely. As a result, the sun's heat is more concentrated over the northern hemisphere, with more of it striking each square metre of ground, giving higher average temperatures at that time of year.

world of science

why do trainers always smell so bad?

That cheesy smell is down to the millions of bacteria from your sweaty foot that become trapped in the trainer. There are more than 200,000 sweat glands in the foot, which pour out sweat at such a rate when you exercise that it can't escape through the trainer fabric. So it just sits there and festers – a germ's paradise. Washing your feet every day, drying properly between your toes and wearing clean socks will help but not cure it, according to experts at Adidas. And they don't recommend putting pongy leather trainers in the washing machine, as it will ruin them.

How many different chemicals are there?

The ability of carbon to form chains means that the number of potential carbon-based combinations is endless. So far, over four million chemicals have been identified and 5,000 new ones are discovered or created every week.

Do disinfectants really kill all known germs?

Apparently so, according to the manufacturers. But their claims can be misleading. If strong disinfectants such as bleach are put directly onto germs in the lab, then yes, they'll kill them all – bacteria and viruses alike. But if you only use warm water and washing-up liquid on the plates once a day, or pour bleach down the loo every week, then forget it: you won't touch the bugs lurking under layers of grease and stuck-on gunge. Bleach stops working after a day or so, anyway. And some disinfectants, including pine-scented fluids, hardly kill anything.

There's only one way to zap all known germs: hard scrubbing with detergent and very hot water to loosen the bacteria, rinsing and dowsing with bleach. Then you'll have a loo that even a hospital would be proud of.

How much electrical power has nuclear fusion generated over the years?

In theory, nuclear fusion is the perfect energy source. Slamming together nuclei of light atoms such as hydrogen and its isotopes so violently that they fuse and release energy, fusion offers essentially limitless supplies of fuel (available from sea-water), little radioactive waste and no greenhouse gases. But in 50 years the attempts to harness this power source that keeps the stars burning have not generated enough electricity to fire up a light bulb.

Billions of pounds have been spent trying to simulate the same conditions that occur in the stars on Earth, but being able to control the reaction long enough to extract the resulting massive burst of energy in a useful form has proved the stumbling block. The temperature needed to fuse hydrogen-like atoms together to produce the necessary nuclear reactions is an incredible 100,000,000°C. The joke among scientists is that "fusion power is 40 years in the future – and it always will be".

Governments are beginning to get a bit fed up with the lack of success. In 1998, America announced that it was effectively abandoning its involvement in the international efforts to harness nuclear fusion. Since then, there's been more chance of generating electricity from all the hot air of scientists involved in the project than from nuclear fusion itself.

Do images in parallel mirrors reflect infinitely?

In theory, yes, although each new reflection would be fractionally slower than the previous one, due to the effect of gravity. In practice however, it is impossible to engineer a perfectly smooth, uniform mirror surface and so with each reflection a small amount of the ray's energy will be scattered by minute flaws in the glass.

The same is true of the "picture within a picture" phenomenon, where a TV newsreader, say, has a television behind him that is tuned to the channel he's broadcasting on. As the picture of him gets smaller and smaller on each screen within another screen, it also degrades due to loss of energy to transmission media such as wires and cables. According to Dr Paul Alexander, a Cambridge physicist: "This is a serious problem in experimental physics – particularly when scientists attempt to devise apparatus to determine the force of gravity on light.

"This tiny effect is only detectable over an enormous distance," he explains, "and this is commonly simulated by bouncing a light ray back and forth between mirrors and then measuring the ray's course deviation after a decent period of time. The mirrors would have to be incredibly well engineered to permit this, though, and so huge sums of money are spent producing them."

what is the most violent phenomenon to have occurred on earth?

Volcanic eruptions, earthquakes and hurricanes all regularly assault our planet, claiming tens of thousands of lives per year. The most violent earthquake recorded happened in Ecuador in 1906. It measured 8.6 on the Richter scale and was the equivalent of 100 H-bombs. That was nothing compared to the largest-ever volcanic eruption – at Tambora in Indonesia in 1815 – which scores a rating equivalent to 10,000 H-bombs.

Yet even these pale into insignificance compared to routine tropical hurricanes: in the space of an hour they can unleash the energy of a staggering 100,000 H-bombs. This is spread over a vast area, but it's still a mighty punch.

There's only one natural phenomenon that can beat all these. The impact of the meteor that is thought to have killed the dinosaurs 65 million years ago is estimated to have delivered the explosive punch of 10 million H-bombs. No wonder they didn't get up again.

Are heights above sea level measured from high tide, low tide or in between?

According to Paul Riley of the Ordnance Survey Office, sea level changes constantly. Not only does the tide go up and down, but the oceans expand and contract with temperature. The sea also dips and rises around the world, causing very shallow peaks and troughs. The British Isles actually lie in a valley about 80cm deep. Because of such variations, countries have their own local mean sea levels, which can vary by as much as two metres from global mean sea level.

Heights in Great Britain are measured from a tide-gauge at Newlyn, Cornwall, where the sea level was taken every hour from 1915 to 1921 to obtain an average. Although tide-gauge measurements are still quoted, all Ordnance Survey work is now done using the more precise Global Positioning System.

What makes the rock inside volcanoes so hot?

In a word – radioactivity. Locked inside the Earth are huge quantities of radioactive uranium, thorium and potassium whose decay heats up the interior of our planet to very high temperatures. The molten core of the earth is approximately 4,000°C, while about 95 per cent of the Earth is at a temperature of over 1,000°C, which is the temperature of most lavas. However, not all lavas are the same – and depending on the nature of the molten rock (mainly basalt or granite), how much gas they contain, and whether they had to follow a direct or long, circuitous route to the surface, they cool at different rates. Some lavas form a thick skin that can actually be walked on within about eight hours, especially those with a lot of gas (usually carbon dioxide) dissolved in them to form a frothy insulating surface.

Where lava flows into the sea, the insulation is so effective that the surrounding water remains relatively cool – even though the lava stays white hot a couple of centimetres under its surface

This insulating property explains why occasionally trees, cars and buildings can be engulfed by a lava flow and seemingly remain unscorched for minutes before finally bursting into flames. That is, of course, providing the superheated gases haven't got to them first.

🔮 why do objects look bigger underwater?

🔵 They look bigger because they look closer. We're used to judging the size and distance of an object on the basis that light is travelling in a straight line. But when light rays pass from water to air they change direction (refraction). By the time they reach your eyes, your brain reckons that they correspond to a closer, bigger object.

The laws of refraction say that underwater objects should look about 33 per cent larger than they are. But our brains often adjust the sizes of images we see and the perception of size can alter with practice. For example, experienced divers are able to judge the underwater world more accurately than novices, and spear fishermen compensate automatically when aiming for their next meal.

🔮 can earthquakes be predicted?

🔵 For over 100 years, scientists have looked for telltale signs called "precursors" that might be relied on to forecast earthquakes. Some have tried to link big quakes with foreshocks, small tremors that might be a sign of an impending release of pent-up seismic energy. Others have put their faith in increases in levels of radioactive radon gas escaping from the soil, or slight changes in the tilt of the ground. Still others have looked for patterns in the timing of big quakes, claiming to see signs of regular cycles.

In 1975, scientists in China stunned the world by apparently succeeding: not just correctly predicting an earthquake, but also saving the lives of thousands by moving them out of the area to safety. On 3 February 1975 a swarm of small quakes struck Haicheng Province in Manchuria. Believing them to be precursors of some far more serious event, Chinese geophysicists issued a warning of a major quake within the next two days. What happened next remains unclear. Some accounts speak of mass evacuations being set in motion, but others have looked in vain for any evidence that they took place. What is clear is that less than a day later, a major quake did strike, registering 7.3 on the Richter scale.

The Haicheng earthquake has been hailed by some seismologists as the first successful prediction of a major quake, and one which saved the lives of thousands. But others remain deeply sceptical, pointing out that the Chinese seismologists had made another prediction some months earlier, based on the same type of precursor – but that quake had failed to materialise.

The continuing lack of a single, unequivocally successful quake forecast has divided the scientific community into those who think quakes are intrinsically unpredictable, and those who believe they can be predicted – given more research, and a lot more funding.

Sceptics point to the growing evidence that earthquakes are "self-organising critical" (SOC) phenomena like avalanches, in which just a tiny disturbance can set off catastrophic changes. If true, this would explain why quake prediction has proved so elusive: it's like guessing which grain of sand will trigger an avalanche on a sand-pile.

Both laboratory simulations and studies of earthquake records support the idea that quakes really are SOC phenomena, and thus essentially unpredictable. But there's another, simpler reason why prediction is so hard: big earthquakes are very rare. Only about once every 50 to 100 years does a major quake strike a city like Tokyo or Los Angeles. As a result, any prediction system runs a grave risk of triggering false alarms – simply because it's far more likely there isn't going to be a quake than that one will strike. Calculations suggest that such a system could only be trusted if it was at least 100 times more reliable than any weather forecast has ever been. So far, however, quake prediction methods have proved little better than tossing a coin.

can buildings be made quakeproof?

An earthquake makes buildings sway from side to side, so engineers have developed systems to dampen out the swaying effects. Some skyscrapers are built on rubber bearings; others have computer-controlled counterweights at the top to cancel out the swaying. But one type of building has survived countless earthquakes: the traditional Japanese pagoda.

Only two of the 500 or so of these wooden structures have collapsed over 1,400 years. Their secret lies in the construction of their floors, which aren't fixed to one another, but can move about; a massive trunk-like pillar in the centre prevents them from breaking free. Once a quake strikes, the floors move but the damaging energy is sent harmlessly to the ground.

can we drink heavy water?

Water is composed of molecules that have two atoms of hydrogen and one of oxygen. There are different kinds (isotopes) of hydrogen: ordinary "light" hydrogen and two "heavy" hydrogens. Water that contains heavy hydrogens is heavy water and not really drinkable.

Isotopes have differing numbers of protons and neutrons in their atomic nuclei. The nucleus of light hydrogen (H) has only one proton, but the heavy hydrogen deuterium (D) has one proton and one neutron, and tritium (T) one proton and two neutrons.

Deuterated water slows down chemical reactions and would do the same to your metabolism. Tritium is much more dangerous – it is radioactive and emits beta particles (electrons that travel close to the speed of light). When beta particles interact with living tissue, they give up their energy causing huge biological damage. High doses of beta particles give you radiation sickness (nausea and vomiting, which may spiral into haemorrhage, convulsions and death).

why does the colour red always signal danger or stop?

On stop signs, brake lights and level crossings around the world, the colour red always means "danger" or "stop". The convention seems to have originated with the old naval signal flag system now used for communication by ships internationally. When ships are engaged in a hazardous activity, such as loading ammunition, they hoist the red flag for danger. So red was also chosen for "stop" when the signals and crossings were built for Britain's nineteenth-century railways and when the first traffic lights were installed in front of the Houses of Parliament in 1868.

There are also sound physiological reasons for choosing red to signify stop or danger. As a primary colour, at the long end of the visible spectrum, red can be seen from further away than any other colour. We may also be sensitive to it because it is also the colour of blood. Experiments have shown that metabolic rate increases by 13 per cent when red is seen and strength of hand-grip increases almost 20 per cent under red lighting.

what is the number one parasite?

Assuming the number one means the most common parasite, the title goes to *Trichinella spiralis*, a type of roundworm. Groups of them, each growing to lengths of 3.5mm, inhabit the intestines of about a quarter of the world's population – that's about 1,500 million people. In extreme cases, hundreds or even thousands of *Trichinellae* may block the gut entirely, or cause bleeding if the larvae migrate to other parts of the body. The tapeworm, *Taenia saginata*, would get an award for the largest human parasite, with individual worms attaining lengths of up to 6m.

If number one is taken to mean the most dangerous, then the rat flea – which is responsible for carrying bubonic plague – or the malarial parasite are both contenders.

How is salt formed?

Salt or halite is a very common mineral that can be found the world over, and its journey from the Earth to your dinner table began millions of years ago. Rich deposits of natural salt were laid down in beds when the planet was submerged beneath shallow prehistoric seas. As time went on, the seas slowly retreated, leaving behind vast salt-water lakes, which were then covered by layers of rocks from other sedimentary deposits.

The beds of halite that lie trapped beneath our feet may range in depth from a few metres to over thirtymetres thick, and can be found very deep below the surface of the Earth. In the UK, halite beds run in a wide band from Northern Ireland, via Cheshire and Cleveland through to the north-eastern coast.

In dry areas, salt tends to accumulate because of high rates of evaporation and limited leaching (where flowing water carries it in solution into the sea). Salt can also appear in the form of "glaciers" where massive reserves migrate to the Earth's surface as a result of the upward "doming" of subterranean salt strata. If the dome pierces the overlying rock or the cap is eroded, the salt deposit will be attached.

As well as being mined in its own right, salt can also be a useful geological marker; petroleum geologists look for salt deposits to lead them to oil and gas. Because of their impervious nature, halite deposits stop oil and gas from escaping, and so form natural underground reservoirs.

What's the closest a comet has come to hitting earth in recent times?

The French astronomer Charles Lexell spotted a comet in June 1770 which was moving at around 140,000 km/h on an apparent collision-course with Earth. Two weeks later, it came within just 2.25 million kilometres of a direct hit, which would have wiped out life on Earth.

Some asteroids – rocks orbiting chiefly between Mars and Jupiter – have come closer. In May 1996 one such heavenly body, code-named JA1, came within 450,000km of Earth. Travelling at 80,000km/hr and measuring 300m across, its impact would have equalled the destructive punch of 3,000 H-bombs. Astronomers are watching for other Potentially Hazardous Asteroids (PHAs), and the next close shave is predicted to occur in October 2086, when an asteroid called Hathor comes within 730,000km of Earth.

ⓆⓉ where is the most likely spot in europe for a major earthquake, and why?

ⒶⓉ The precise mechanics of earthquakes remain elusive. A few years back, Stanford geophysicist Mark Zoback wrote: "We fundamentally do not understand how earthquakes work. After all these years, we still don't have a clue." However, it is definitely known that earthquakes are connected with build-ups of tension along continental plate boundaries, making these areas a great deal more prone to earthquakes, both minor and major.

In Europe, such seismic zones are found at the boundaries of the Eurasian plate with the African and Hellenic plates, located along the Mediterranean and Black Sea coasts and taking in cities including Athens, Ankara, Bucharest, Lisbon, Milan, Naples and Rome. Quakes are also comparatively common around the mountain regions of the Alps and Pyrenees, where the geological layers are stressed and cracked by the upthrusting mountains.

Every day, so many minor earthquakes occur in southern Europe that in Italy they are listed daily on Teletext. The most probable spot for a major earthquake is in these zones, but seismologists are unable to predict exactly where, and are temperamentally averse to guessing.

Not that people living outside seismic zones should relax: there are between 300 and 400 earth tremors detected in Britain every year. One in 1990 reached 5.2 on the Richter scale.

🔵 can forecasters predict weather years ahead?

🔴 Meteorologists concede that they can't produce reliable weather forecasts for more than about 10 days ahead. The problem lies in the fact that just small errors in the measurements used as the basis of a forecast are rapidly amplified, quickly ruining accuracy – a phenomenon known as the Butterfly Effect, according to which the flap of a butterfly's wing in Kansas can trigger a typhoon over Singapore.

But that doesn't mean that scientists can't tell us what the great British climate will be doing next year: it's a safe bet that on average it'll be colder in December than in July. This highlights the difference between climate – the broad pattern of weather – and weather itself, which is what is thrown at us on a daily basis.

Scientists have, however, found evidence that they might be able to do a bit better than this. They have found a link between the temperature of the Atlantic and an atmospheric effect known as the North Atlantic Oscillation (NAO), which flips between two different states: one gives warm and wet winters in Europe, the other gives dry and cold winters.

In 1999, climate modellers at the Meteorological Office, Bracknell, found that knowing the temperature of the surface of the Atlantic allowed them to predict the right NAO state two times out of three, with the hit-rate for extreme NAOs reaching three times out of four. As researchers already think they can predict these ocean temperatures fairly accurately several years in advance, this suggests that it might be possible to predict the NAO state – and thus the type of winter weather over Europe – several years ahead as well.

🔵 why is it always windy near skyscrapers?

🔴 The reason for this is that skyscrapers act like giant sails, diverting the winds that blow unfelt over our heads down to the ground. Because there's not much to slow them down up there, these winds can be three times the speed of those at ground level. Once they slam into a skyscraper, they shoot down and strike the ground at its base to form powerful vortices that curl up and over. These are what tear our hats off our heads and our umbrellas out of our hands. In winter, the vortices can also create extreme wind-chill effects.

what makes sliced apple turn brown?

Once cut open, the inside of the apple is exposed to the surrounding air, triggering oxidation of tannic acid, a chemical in apples which gives them their slightly acidic taste. When combined with oxygen, tannic acid turns into so-called polyphenol compounds, which are brown in colour – this is why the longer the apple slice is left exposed to the air, the browner it goes. With tannic acid being common in many edible fruits and vegetables, supermarkets wanting to keep their produce looking fresh have developed packaging filled with special gases which slow down the discolouration reaction.

what are "supervolcanoes"?

Forget asteroids, scientists have recently asked the government to look into what they believe to be a much bigger danger to the human race – supervolcanoes and the threat of a "volcanic winter". A report from the Geological Society says these supervolcanoes, of which there are at least four in existence, could cause global devastation and wipe out the human race. Supervolcanoes are formed from a huge pool of magma that gathers beneath the Earth's surface. The pressure of the gases in the molten rock builds up until the magma blasts through the Earth from several points with 100 times more force than any normal eruption. Only the Caldera – the subsided crater of the magma chamber – is left, like a huge valley.

Yellowstone Park is a massive Caldera. At 43 by 18 miles in area it is the world's largest single active volcano system. Until recently, scientists thought the supervolcano here was extinct; now they have estimated the times of the last three eruptions: 2m years ago, 1.2m years ago and 600,000 years ago – so we could be due one any day. The eruption of a supervolcano would shoot a column of ash and gas high into the stratosphere, releasing sulphur dioxide. On contact with water droplets in the atmosphere, this would become sulphuric acid, which would reflect the sun's rays and cool the Earth's temperature. The resulting crop failures would mean worldwide famine.

Some genetics experts claim that this has already happened. Around 74,000 years ago, the global population was reduced to 70,000 people, which resulted in a decrease in variation in human DNA. The last supervolcanic eruption (Lake Toba in Sumatra) was nearly 74,000 years ago. Coincidence?

Professor Bill McGuire, director of Hazard Research at University College, London, and author of *Apocalypse: A natural history of global disasters*, says of the likelihood of supervolcano events: "You would get a lot of prior activity as a warning, but it might occur in a poorly inhabited area, somewhere we're not even monitoring. I'm 100 per cent certain it will happen. Natural disasters have already virtually wiped out the planet's population in the past. In the worst case scenario, it could be like night for two years and there would be global starvation. Statistically we are overdue one, but luckily for us, nature doesn't necessarily work that way."

Is it possible to grow human skin in the lab?

Yes. The first commercially available product in the world of human engineered tissues was launched recently – to treat foot ulcers. The laboratory-developed skin was originally grown from the bits thrown away after circumcising newborn babies.

It's made by creating a fine frame from the polymer thread used for stitching wounds and then planting skin cells into it. The cells grow across the mesh, which eventually dissolves, and the skin can then be cut to the shape of the wound. Bags of skin cells are also used in "living bandages" that can be applied to severe burns, helping the body's own skin to heal more quickly.

Other growth areas in the science of tissue engineering are ligaments, bone and cartilage; a recent breakthrough was a lab-grown human ear. Now researchers are looking at the ultimate challenge – making home-grown joints for hip replacements.

what makes whips "crack"?

The noise is actually a mini sonic boom. Shake any piece of cord violently, and you'll send a wave-like swirl down its length. You won't usually get a "crack", though, as the wave isn't travelling fast enough. You will with a whip, however, as it gets thinner down its length. As a result, the energy of the initial shaking is injected into an ever-lighter part of the whip, which thus moves ever faster. By the time it reaches the fine tip of the whip, the wave is travelling faster than the speed of sound, triggering a cracking sonic boom. All of which explains what every naughty schoolchild knows: you have to coil up a wet towel or tie so that it tapers at one end to stand a chance of getting a resounding smack when it hits the backside of your victim.

would you be weightless at the Earth's centre?

This is a question that Sir Isaac Newton himself had to wrestle with after coming up with his law of gravity. Solving the problem required some pretty heavyweight mathematics, but the upshot is simple enough. Wherever you are on the Earth – beyond, on or inside it – you will feel the force of gravity generated by whatever mass is between you and the centre of the Earth.

Consequently, if you were just an infinitesimal dot sitting at the precise centre of the Earth, then it is true that you would be weightless. It wouldn't be much fun, however, because you would still have to deal with all that molten rock and iron above you, pressing down under the pull of gravity. But in practice, everything does possess dimensions, so you would still feel some gravity.

why does water pour well out of some containers, and dribble out of others?

No matter how carefully you try to pour liquids out of some glasses, it seems you always ends up with the liquid clinging to the side and pouring on to the table. The problem is that as the liquid pours out, a zone of low pressure forms on its lower surface – allowing the pressure of the surrounding air to curl it under the rim and dribble down the side. Surprisingly, you stand more chance of avoiding dribbles if you don't pour out the liquid gingerly, but to do it briskly – giving it enough momentum to overcome the pressure effect.

A specially-shaped spout can certainly help, by delivering enough liquid fast enough to avoid dribbles. In 1998, design student Damini Kumar at London's South Bank University patented a teapot with a special grooved spout which she claims virtually rules out the risk of dribbling.

How does the osmosis pump that aircrew use for survival when downed in the sea work?

If you have two different liquid solutions – say, sea-water and fresh water – separated by a semi-permeable membrane, molecules will seep across the membrane until the density on each side becomes the same. This molecular smoothing-out process is called osmosis – and by reversing it, clean, fresh water can be generated from sea-water.

Such reverse osmosis demands that pressure is applied to force the sea-water across the semi-permeable membrane, dumping all of its dissolved salts to leave just fresh water on the other side. Around 70 atmospheres of pressure are needed, but survival kits include hand-pumps that can reach such high pressures. With even the smallest viruses being unable to get through the membrane, the resulting water is incredibly pure, and tastes like distilled water.

History,
mystery
and culture

where did Guy Fawkes go wrong?

For a start it's pretty unlikely that the House of Lords would have gone up in smoke, even if Guy Fawkes hadn't been caught red-handed on 4 November 1605. The reason? It's now thought that the gunpowder Fawkes and his men were using was so damp, and such low quality that the net effect would have been, quite literally, a damp squib. A better question might be why was Fawkes involved in a plot to blow up King James I and his government in the first place?

It was all to do with religion: Fawkes was a member of a group of Catholics called the Recusants, which formed the majority of the men behind the plot. Most of the plotters were quickly captured, then hanged, drawn and quartered for treason. Interestingly, Guy Fawkes was born a Protestant and converted to Catholicism after his mother married a Recusant. When he was caught, he initially told his captors that his name was John Johnson, but later, under torture, confessed that it wasn't.

what inspired the Book of Revelations?

There's a theory that says that the "Antichrist" figure central to the *Book of Revelations* is actually Nero. This competent fiddler was forced to stab himself in the throat in AD68 but was popularly expected to return from the dead with an army from the east to fight to regain his throne. *The Book of Revelations'* vicious attacks on Rome suggest that it was written – possibly by the John who wrote the fourth Gospel – just after the massacre of the Christians in the last years of Nero's reign, and after the Jewish War in AD60.

There is another small fact that some think adds weight to the theory – if you give the Hebrew letters for Nero Caesar numerical values they add up to 666.

(Q) Are we any nearer to discovering the lost world of Atlantis?

(A) The Legend of Atlantis dates back at least as far as the Greek philosopher Plato who claimed almost 2,400 years ago that Atlantis was once an island lying "beyond the Pillars of Hercules", now known as the Straits of Gibraltar. Its inhabitants were supposedly great and powerful, but both they and their beautiful city were said to have drowned following an earthquake around 9600BC.

Archaeologists have found evidence at various sites for an Atlantis-like culture that met with disaster. Some of these fit Plato's description quite well but most of them do not. Many researchers think that Plato got his geography wrong, and that the real Atlantis was the ancient Minoan civilisation of Crete. Around 1600BC, the volcanic island of Thera – now called Santorini – exploded, creating a vast tsunami estimated to have been around 90 metres high, which engulfed nearby Crete. Other researchers, notably the Russian Viatcheslav Koudriavtsev, claim that Atlantis was further north – he believes that it may have been just off the southern tip of Cornwall.

Impressive backing for Plato's original siting of Atlantis emerged in 1996, following tests on apparently man-made stone found on the seabed near the island of Bimini in the Bahamas. The link between Bimini and Atlantis first emerged in 1968, when a local diver discovered a mysterious J-shaped "road" of closely-packed stones off the island's north-west coast. An archaeological expedition in the same area in 1975 found man-made stones with a sophisticated tongue and groove joint system, and marble pillars, the like of which had never been seen in the Bahamas. In 1996, tests by scientists from the UK Building Research Establishment near Watford found tiny amounts of gold in samples taken from the site.

Sceptics have argued that the pillars may be nothing more than decorations that were intended for the homes of rich plantation-owners in America, but became lost in wrecks. However, tests on the samples revealed evidence of so-called "cement clinker", which suggests that the stones were made sometime before the 1820s, when the modern "Portland cement" process was invented.

🔹 what happened to the little girl in that famous picture of her fleeing her village in vietnam?

🔹 The little girl in the picture is called Phan Thi Kim Phuc. She was nine years old when she was photographed escaping from Tramg Bang near Saigon, which had been hit by a napalm attack. After taking his photo (which later won a Pulitzer prize), the photographer, Nick Ut, took Kim to hospital, where it took her 14 months to recover from the burns covering her body. Kim later fled to Canada where, at 37, she still lives with her husband and two children.

In 1997, UNESCO made Kim a goodwill ambassador for Vietnam, and recently she attended the opening of an exhibition of Nick Ut's work at the Science Museum in London. Entitled "The Making of the Modern World", it featured the famous picture, taken on 8 June 1972, and the camera Ut used to take it.

🔹 is it true that eskimos have hundreds of different words for snow?

🔹 This is one of those great urban myths that has a grain of truth in it. It's true that the Inuit language used by most Eskimos has many ways of describing snow, but all of them are made from just four basic roots: *aput* (snow on the ground), *gana* (falling snow), *piqsirpoq* (drifting snow), and *qimuqsuq* (a snow drift). You could boost the number somewhat by including other Eskimo languages, but the figure never reaches anything like hundreds. A count of snow-related entries in Eskimo dictionaries puts the figure at around 24 – which sounds impressive until one counts up the snow-related words in English, which easily exceeds thirty.

A similar myth has arisen over the Greek language, which is said to have four different words for love. A romantic notion, no doubt, but one that doesn't hold much water. However, a study by Steve DeRose at Brown University in the USA identified 19 different English words for varieties of love, ranging from adoration to lust.

The fact is that the English language has a greater number of words than any other language in the world and so is much better equipped to pin down any concept with precision.

Did Jesus really exist?

You don't have to take the word of Christians on this one: in their own records, the Romans themselves mention a "trouble-maker" called Jesus in the Holy Land.

The historian Tacitus, writing about 70 years after the supposed death of Christ, records the existence of a group of people called "Christians" on whom the Emperor Nero blamed the burning of Rome in AD64.

"The name," Tacitus explains, "comes from Christ, whom the procurator Pontius Pilate had executed in the reign of Tiberius." He goes on to describe how this Christ character had created a "temporarily suppressed pernicious superstition" in Judea, which eventually spread across the Empire to Rome itself.

What happened when Christianity reached Rome is briefly described by another historian, Suetonius, in his biography of the Emperor Claudius, also written around AD100. According to Suetonius, a man called "Chrestus" has stirred up so much discontent among the Jews that Claudius decided to evict all of then from Rome, just to be on the safe side.

Various other passing references to Jesus appear in Roman literature of the era. Josephus, historian to the Emperor Domitian, talks of a man called James, "the brother of Jesus, who was called Christ".

In short, as much as we can be sure about anything that went on 2000 years ago, there was a man named Jesus who lived in the Holy Land sometime between AD26 and AD36 and his followers caused an awful lot of trouble for the Romans later on.

💬 who was Hamlet in real life?

🅐 The short answer is no one. The story of the Great Dane, or Prince of Denmark, has its origins in a popular Icelandic saga mentioned by Snaebjörn, an Icelandic poet of the tenth century. The name Hamlet was probably drawn from Amleth, a character in a twelfth-century account of early Danish history by the chronicler Saxo Grammaticus. This tells how Horvendill, the father of Amleth, is killed by his own brother Feng, who then marries Gerutha, the widow of his victim. As so often with his plays, Shakespeare seems to have borrowed the basic plot from this pre-existing story, turning Amleth into Hamlet, Feng into Claudius and Gerutha into Gertrude.

While Hamlet may never have actually existed, his predicament – of having to take difficult decisions but lacking the strength of character to see them through – is real enough, and Shakespeare's most demanding character has been brought to life by some of the world's greatest actors: Laurence Olivier, Richard Burton, Ben Kingsley, Mel Gibson, Kenneth Branagh – and Sarah Bernhardt.

💬 why, when we drive on the left in Britain, do we stand on the right-hand side of escalators?

🅐 No one seems to know for sure, but the London Transport Museum suggests that it might be because when LT's first escalators were introduced you stepped onto them sideways and from the left. After leading with your right foot, it would be natural to continue moving onto the right.

London Transport's "keep right" rule on the underground leaves a convenient fast lane on the left for commuters in a hurry. "But you aren't really supposed to walk or run up escalators as it can cause accidents," says LT's Neil Byrne.

In fact, more than one-fifth of the accidents on the Underground which require hospital treatment happen on escalators and in lifts. There are about 150 every year. Slips, trips and falls are common. "Tourists reading maps, people walking down escalators reading books, getting off backwards while chatting to the person behind, I've seen it all," says Byrne philosophically.

what is the longest place name on earth?

Well, believe it or not, it's not that Welsh tongue twister Llanfairpwllgwyngyllgogerychwyrndrobwllllantysiliogogogoch, the name of a village in Anglesey. At 58 letters it is barely a third of the length of the world's longest place name – Bangkok.

The official name of the capital of Thailand is Kerugtep Mahanakhan. However, this is only a much shortened version of its older title – Krungthep Mahanakhon Amornratanakosin Mahinthara Ayutthaya Mahadilok Phopnoppharat Ratchathani Burirom Udomratchaniwet Mahasathan Amornphiman Awatanasathit Sakkathathiya Witsanukamprasit – which has a total of 172 letters.

Vying for first place in the shortest name stakes, meanwhile, are Y (pronounced E) in France and Å in Norway. As for Llanfairpwllgwyngyllgogerychwyrndrobwllllantysiliogogogoch, tongue-tied north Welshmen now refer to it simply as Llanfair PG. The name means, incidentally: "St Mary's church in a hollow by the white hazel, close to the rapid whirlpool, by the red cave of St Tysilio", which is 84 letters long, making the Welsh version seem almost snappy.

History, mystery and culture

🔘 was there a single day of peace in the twentieth century?

🔘 No. The Department of War Studies at the Sandhurst Academy defines war as: "The employment of structured violence between two or more entities in pursuit of political aims." The word "structured" is used to distinguish between the violence of a lone terrorist and the actions of a group such as ETA, the Basque separatist movement. "Entities" covers everything from a super-power to the army of an independent warlord. And "politics" includes economic, territorial, cultural, racial and ideological aims.

Using this definition, there wasn't a single day of peace in the whole century. In fact, there were at least 200 wars. If you include major riots and insurrections, the figure rises to more than 500.

How many people were killed in these conflicts through direct military action or through disease or starvation is more difficult to quantify. A very conservative estimate is 200 million, which includes 20 million from World War I and 170 million from World War II.

Oddly enough, the number of wars in which a given number of people are killed follows a mathematical law, established over 70 years ago by an English physicist, Lewis Fry Richardson.

In his book *The Statistics of Deadly Quarrels*, Richardson attempted to bring together, in as objective a form as possible, data on all wars from 1820 onward. Plotting a graph of the numbers of wars against the death-toll "magnitudes" (calculated by converting the raw figure into logarithms), Richardson made a surprising discovery: they followed a straight line. At its extremes, the straight line follows the commonsense expectation that there have been relatively few wars producing huge death-tolls, with skirmishes resulting in several thousand deaths being far more common. But, strikingly, conflicts between these two extremes also lie on the same straight line. Mathematicians believe that Richardson's "Law of War" reflects the fact that there's no way of telling whether a dispute will produce a skirmish or a massive conflict.

🅠 Did Moses cross the Red Sea?

🅐 The Old Testament Book of Exodus describes how Moses led his people out of slavery in Egypt via the Red Sea, which conveniently parted for the crossing, and then closed again when the Pharaoh's troops tried to follow, drowning them all.

Though relatively narrow, the Red Sea plunges to a depth of almost 3km in some places, enough to give even miracle-workers a very long pause for thought.

However, the stretch of the Red Sea next to Egypt – the Gulf of Suez – is a mere 70 metres deep. While it would undoubtedly take a miracle to walk through it now, one explanation for Moses' feat could be that major geological and climatic changes have taken place over the 3,500 years since he and his followers made their escape. It is just possible that back then this part of the Red Sea was, like the English Channel and the Bering Straits, so shallow that people could walk across it, so long as they knew the right path. Presumably Moses, or his guide, did and the Pharaoh's chaps didn't.

An alternative explanation of the miracle has been put forward by an Australian Christian fundamentalist explorer called Jonathan Geray. He claims that the crossing took place at the Gulf of Aqaba, between Saudi Arabia and the Sinai Peninsula. He bases his claims on video footage taken of the sea bed in that area, which allegedly show eight-spoke wheels of the type used by the pharaohs of Egypt around the time Moses lived.

🅠 How many bricks are there in the Great Wall of China?

🅐 Nobody knows for certain. The wall, which is around 4,000 miles long and around 30ft high, is not made of brick alone, but from a mixture of hardened earth, stone and brick, built and added to over the centuries by different emperors. It has been estimated that the basic wall, which was begun in 3BC, contains enough stone to build another eight-foot high wall that could circle the globe. It's unlikely that anyone will try doing this, though, as it took five Chinese dynasties to build the original, which remains the largest man-made structure in the world. Incidentally, although the Great Wall of China can be seen from "space" you can't see it from the Moon: it may be long, but it's only around 20 feet wide, making it too narrow to be seen by the naked eye from so great a distance.

why did Lady Godiva ride on horseback naked?

Lady Godiva was a real person, although Godiva is a modern version of her actual name, which was Godgifu. An Anglo-Saxon woman, she lived in Coventry with her husband, Leofric, earl of Mercia, and founded a monastery there in 1043. According to a thirteenth-century historian, Godgifu performed her famous ride in 1057 for a bet. Fed up with her constant pleadings to reduce the taxes imposed on the people of Coventry, Leofric promised to do as she asked – if she rode naked through the town on a white horse. Godgifu stunned him by agreeing, forcing Leofric to keep to his part of the bargain.

While there are no recorded eye-witness accounts of the ride, investigations commissioned by King Edward I seem to support the story by revealing the strange taxation anomaly that appeared at the time Godgifu lived in Coventy. It is such a good tale that others have not been able to resist embellishing it. The story about Godiva having her blushes spared by her long, flowing locks was added during the seventeenth century – along with the legend of Peeping Tom, who was struck blind after glimpsing the full beauty of the lady. Both seem to reflect Puritan prudery rather than historical fact.

Lady Godiva is still fondly remembered in Coventry. A statue commemorating her tax-cutting ride has pride of place near St Michael's Cathedral.

Is it true that the statue of Liberty wasn't built in America?

Yes, it is. The monument that has come to symbolise all things American was actually built in France – it was a gift to the US to celebrate the friendship established between the countries in the American Revolution.

The statue was scaled up from the designs of sculptor Frederic-Auguste Bartholdi. Bartholdi was assisted by Gustave Eiffel, who addressed the structural issues involved in erecting such a colossal copper monument. Eiffel designed an internal iron pylon that runs the length of the statue and the skeletal structure beneath Liberty's surface. Funding problems meant the statue wasn't completed in time for the centenary of American Independence in 1876. Liberty arrived in New York in 1886 aboard the frigate *Isere*, in 350 separate pieces in 214 crates. Assembled, she now overlooks New York harbour and stands 92.9m high from the ground to the tip of her torch.

How old is sign language and is there a global system?

Contrary to popular belief, sign language is not universal. There is a universal system – Gestuno – but it is not widely used. Many different systems have evolved and they show just as much variation around the world as spoken languages, right down to regional dialects. Even some countries that share the same spoken language – such as the US and UK – have distinct sign languages. The earliest record of gestural communication between the deaf occurs in the Hebrew text of the Talmud. But its presence among Australian Aborigines and Kalahari Bush people suggests that it may date from prehistoric times.

British sign language has been used for hundreds of years. The first pamplet for its use was printed by John Bulwer in 1644.

what makes civilisations collapse?

Civilisations end for a number of reasons. Some go through a long slow decline and finally fade away, others end suddenly and catastrophically. In around 1600BC the island of Thera exploded in a volcanic eruption, wiping out the nearby Minoan civilisation of Crete, which had survived before that for 1,500 years. Invasion can be almost as swift in its destruction. It took just a few decades for the Spanish conquistadors to put an end to the vast Inca empire, which had previously flourished for more than four centuries.

Civilisations that have disappeared dramatically include the Anasazi who lived in what is now the American south-west. They turned from a hunter-gatherer lifestyle to farming in the 6th century AD. At first they flourished but, from 1125 onwards, droughts and famine led to mass migration, leading to the culture's eventual decline. Another example is the city of Mashkan-shikir in Mesopotamia, where the inhabitants had an irrigation system linking the Tigris and Euphrates rivers. Scientists believe that Mashkan-shikir ended up poisoning its own fields. The fields were lower than the river levels and there was no drainage. The water evaporated, leaving mineral salt deposits which by 2300BC had ruined the soil.

why is 13 thought to be an unlucky number?

Studies suggest that around 1 in 10 people are affected by triskaidekaphobia – a fear of the number 13. Certainly many famous people have suffered from a phobia of the number, according to Dr Thomas Fernsler of Mansfield University in Pennsylvania – arguably the world's leading expert on the subject. Napoleon Bonaparte, Herbert Hoover, Mark Twain and Richard Wagner were all triskaidekaphobes, with the German composer having several key events in his life – including his birth (1813), and death (13 February 1883) linked to the number 13. Franklin

Roosevelt, the great American president, had a particularly severe case, inviting his secretary to attend lunch or dinner parties if a cancellation or late addition threatened to put 13 around the table. He also avoided going on visits on the thirteenth of the month, either departing a little before midnight on the previous day, or a little after on the following one.

The prejudice against the number 13 is usually blamed on the Last Supper, where the thirteenth diner was Judas Iscariot. Even today, dining at a table of 13 people is said to be very unlucky; (the world-famous Savoy Hotel goes so far as to seat a large black wooden cat at any table of 13 diners to make the number up to 14). One possibility is that the superstition originated with the ancient Egyptians, to whom the thirteenth step was the last of the ladder by which the soul reached eternity.

Triskaidekaphobia shows little signs of dying out: anyone using the lifts in the ultra-modern Canary Wharf tower block will find it impossible to go to the thirteenth floor – the buttons mysteriously jump from 12 to 14. And even now, you can find people who make a lot out of the fact that Apollo 13 was launched on 11 April 1970 (sum of 1, 1, 4 , 7 and 0 equals 13) from Pad 39 (3 times 13) at 13:13 local time, and was hit by an explosion on April 13.

The bad news for people who find Friday the 13th hard to deal with is that the thirteenth of the month is more likely to fall on a Friday than any other day of the week, a result first proved in 1969 by the mathematician S.R. Baxter at the age of 13 (what else?).

who was the last Japanese soldier to surrender after world war II?

Japan officially surrendered on 2 September 1945, but for some of its troops the war continued for years after that. In March 1974, 2nd Lt. Hiroo Onoda, who had been posted to the Phillipines in December 1944, emerged from the jungle of Lubang Island with his .25 calibre rifle, 500 rounds of ammunition and several hand grenades. He had been declared legally dead by his country in 1959.

But his devotion to duty was later eclipsed by Captain Fumio Nakahira, who was found at Mt. Halcon in Mindoro in the Philippines in April 1980 – almost 35 years after the war had ended. He had remained at his post for so long because he believed that the war was on such a vast scale it would never end. Cut off from the rest of the world in his lonely posting, there had been no one to tell him otherwise.

will the leaning tower of Pisa fall over?

Not for several centuries, at least – thanks to the work of Professor John Burland of London's Imperial College. He is the soil mechanics expert who rescued the 825-year-old, 60-metre high tower tower, allowing it to be re-opened to tourists in the summer of 2001 after a decade of work. He arrived just in the nick of time. When restoration work was begun in 1999, the tower's top cornice overhung the bottom by about 5 metres, and the whole building was gradually tipping over. An even more urgent worry was that the ancient marble cladding on the tower's sinking south side would suddenly explode under the ever-increasing strain. Professor Burland and his colleagues believed they had only a few years at most to save the historic monument.

Building began on the tower in August 1173. The original builders only got as far as the fourth storey before calling a halt, having discovered that the sandy ground was not up to the job, and their impressive tower had sunk a little and was no longer on the level. When work restarted almost a century later, the builders tried to compensate for the northward tilt by putting the higher storeys on slightly askew. Their attempt to defy gravity can still be seen as a slight bend in the tower, just below its half-way point. They too had to stop, however, leaving the banana-shaped tower leaning further than ever, this time southwards. Then in 1360, someone decided to add a bell-tower at the top – and the hundreds of extra tons of iron and marble made the whole tower lurch southward, more than doubling its angle of tilt in just a matter of weeks.

It took the skills of twentieth century science to undo the results of years of cowboy builders, with Professor Burland and his team gently bringing the tower back from the brink by removing tiny quantities of soil from beneath it. Now it has settled back under its own weight about 30cms, into a more stable, and less stressful, position. There are no plans to make the tower perpendicular however – not least because tourists are hardly likely to flock to the Perfectly Vertical Tower of Pisa.

whatever happened to the Bermuda Triangle?

Back in the 1970s the Bermuda Triangle was the subject of countless books and TV programmes. But today it seems to be all but forgotten.

The theory was that there was a patch of ocean, linking Puerto Rico in the south, Miami in the northwest and Bermuda in the east, where boats and planes mysteriously disappeared. But, as stories of unexplained phenomena go, this was a pretty pathetic one, at least according to Mike Hutchinson, co-author of the book *Bizarre Beliefs*. "It still occasionally crops up. But it is basically a non-mystery," he says.

Many stories about "disappearances" of boats in the Bermuda Triangle were so wide of the mark that it took a huge distortion of the facts in order to include them. Not only did many of the "incidents" occur hundreds of miles from the area but, according to a local coastguard, there was a completely logical explanation for almost every case – usually severe weather conditions. This hasn't put a stop to the crazed theories, however. In 1992, an *Equinox* documentary on British TV's Channel 4 put forward the idea of strange gases under the ocean that suck boats under. Says Hutchinson: "I don't think there is any point even considering it when there's no mystery in the first place."

who was the "man in the iron mask"?

Made famous 150 years ago by the novel by Alexander Dumas, the Man in the Iron Mask undoubtedly existed – although there's no evidence he wore anything other than a cloth mask to hide his identity. The mystery man was kept prisoner at various top-security French jails from around 1681 until his death in the notorious Bastille on 19 November 1703.

Many theories about the man's true identity have been put forward – such as his being the disinherited twin brother of Louis XIV. But the name of the most likely candidate emerged in the 1890s, when French military codebreakers deciphered a secret letter written by François de Louvois, Louis XIV's minister for war. This revealed that General Vivien de Bulonde, commander of the French forces near the border with Italy, had been charged with cowardice after leaving his men in the face of possible attack by Austrian troops. The secret message showed that the king had personally demanded his imprisonment – and that de Bulonde was to wear a mask whenever he was out of his cell.

who invented the crossword?

The first ever crossword was introduced to readers of the *New York World* on 21 December 1913. The idea was thought up by Arthur Wynne who was employed in the newspaper's Tricks and Jokes Department. Wynne, who was born in Liverpool, developed the concept from a game called Magic Squares that his grandmother had taught him. The clues to the first puzzles were not difficult, consisting mainly of straightforward word definitions, and were, in fact, similar to the "quick" crosswords that you find in a great number of newspapers today.

It was another 12 years before the cryptic crossword came along, appearing in the now-defunct English newspaper, the *Saturday Westminster*. The originator of these cryptic crosswords is known only by his pseudonym Torquemada, a reference to the Inquisitor General of the Spanish Inquisition, notorious for devising particularly cruel tortures. The cryptic style, which included anagrams, acronyms, encryptions, classical allusions and even the odd cricketing term was taken up by *The Times*, which published its first crossword on 1 February 1930. Compiled by Adrian Bell, early *Times* crosswords also appeared in Latin and Greek to conform with the highbrow affectations of the paper's readers. Today, most crosswords are compiled by computer.

where are the world's oldest cave-paintings?

The oldest prehistoric art discovered so far is located inside the Chauvet cave in the Ardèche region of southern France. This cave was first explored in 1994 and carbon dating of the wall paintings found inside it eventually showed them to be around 32,000 years old. The discovery was a major shock to anthropologists as the art not only pre-dated all previous finds, but was also of a higher standard.

The paintings are considerably more advanced than many that were produced several millennia later, placing in doubt the belief that the artistic ability of prehistoric humans developed in a straightforward linear fashion. The images portrayed on the walls are mainly of animals from the Ice Age. Other discoveries within the cave include a footprint, which is believed to have been made by a 10-year-old boy some 25,000 years ago. The cave has been closed to the general public since the paintings' discovery to prevent any damage to them.

In 1997, archaeologists added to our knowledge of prehistoric art by discovering the world's oldest news story. In Catalhoyuk, southern Turkey, a wall painting was found that had been made to record a volcanic eruption that took place 9,000 years ago.

History, mystery and culture

where does the term "donkey's years" come from?

The phrase basically means "for a very long time" which is something of a puzzle because there is nothing extraordinary about the length of a donkey's life. *Brewer's Phrase and Fable* says the phrase was originally "not for donkey's ears", referring to the length of the donkey's ears, and was mispronounced as "Not for donkey's years." The nonsensical corrupt version thrived at the expense of the original.

whose head is on the sphinx?

Most Egyptologists believe that it is that of Chephren – a pharaoh from the fourth dynasty – although a few dissenters claim it's actually his father, King Chepos. The head on the Sphinx is the spitting image of another statue known to be of Chephren, so all in all it's a pretty good bet that it's him.

The 4,500-year-old Sphinx stands in front of Chephren's burial site – the second of the three great pyramids at Giza – and was the ingenious solution to a minor eyesore that confronted the ancient Egyptians. The place where the Sphinx now stands was originally a stubborn outcrop of rock that marred the view.

The lion's body on the Sphinx symbolises the pharaoh's power and majesty. As for the lack of a nose, legend has it that it was knocked off by Napoleon's soldiers during target practice. It's a good story, but archaeological evidence suggests that the nose actually went missing as early as the Middle Ages, 500 years before Napoleon was born. The most likely explanation is a lot more mundane. According to the British Museum, the nose is the most vulnerable part of most statues and usually the first bit to fall off.

what is the latest theory on the whereabouts of the Lost Ark?

Raiders of the Lost Ark may have been fiction, but it was right about one thing; a lot of people have tried to track down the lost vessel containing the Ten Commandments given to Moses by God. The Ark of the Covenant, said to hold the stone tablets, is meant to confer invincibility to the armies of any country that possesses it, so interest in tracking it down has always been intense.

In 1992, the journalist Graham Hancock published a book claiming that he had discovered the Ark in a mediaeval church at Azum, in Ethiopia. He reported meeting the monk who guarded the chapel, a man called Gebra Makail. Makail refused to let Hancock see the Ark or even describe it, though Hancock later witnessed a replica being carried around in a religious procession. How did it get there? Tradition says that Solomon's son Menelik stole it from him and took it to Ethiopia. Ancient scripts, however, maintain that the Ark was still in Jerusalem hundreds of years after Solomon's death – some believe that it's hidden on Mount Nebo, near Sinai.

The latest theory to appear is that the Ark was hidden under Jerusalem's main temple when Babylonians took the city in 586BC. Recent excavations at Jerusalem's Temple Mount have uncovered a possible secret chamber under the Dome of the Rock in the Western wall and some believe that this is where the Ark will eventually be found.

why was the Black Death so-called, and why did it vanish?

The name is supposed to be derived from the victims' black, putrefying flesh which immediately preceded death. The problem with this theory is that the flesh didn't actually turn black. Indeed, the term "Black Death" wasn't widely used until the early nineteenth century, some 500 years after the first epidemic, which killed at least 75 million in Europe. Black Death may be a mistranslation of the fourteenth-century Latin term *atra mors*, which originally meant "terrible death" but *atra* can also be translated as "black".

Mystery also surrounds the demise of the Black Death as a mass killer. Better sanitation and the decline of the black rat (the fleas of which transmitted the disease) are often suggested as explanations, but neither coincided with the disappearance of the plague. In 1992, historian Dr Kari Konkola of the University of Wisconsin put forward perhaps the most compelling explanation to date. During the latter half of the seventeenth century, mines in Germany started to produce large amounts of arsenic – which happens to be a highly effective rat poison. As its use spread, the appearance of rats in houses decreased and with the rats went the deadly epidemic they carried.

who was the Pied Piper of Hamelin?

According to Robert Browning's 1842 poem, the Pied Piper was a curiously dressed flute-playing pest controller, who rid a medieval Westphalian town (now in Germany) of a plague of rats for an agreed fee of 1000 guilders. Having seen the rats lured to their death in the river Weser, Hamelin's mayor and corporation reneged on the deal. The piper then used the same technique to persuade the town's children to follow him up a nearby mountain, where they disappeared for ever into a magical cave.

The tale probably originates from a real outbreak of the bubonic plague in the town of Hamelin, which then got mixed up with the Children's Crusade of 1212. The Children's Crusade saw 40,000 German youngsters, led by a charismatic teenager called Nicholas, set off over the Alps to rescue the Holy City of Jerusalem from the infidel. Few of the children survived the journey and even fewer ever returned. Most were captured and sold into slavery.

🔮 I'd like an unusual burial – any suggestions?

🔬 On 21 April 1997, the ashes of 24 people, including *Star Trek* creator Gene Roddenberry and psychedelic drugs guru Timothy Leary, were shot into orbit. And on 31 July 1999, Dr Eugene Shoemaker (of Shoemaker-Levy comet fame) became the first man to be "buried" on the moon. A capsule containing his ashes was carried on board the NASA Lunar Prospector mission and fired onto the Moon's surface near the lunar south pole.

Sending human remains into space has now become big business. A Houston-based firm, Celestis Inc, will fill a lipstick-sized capsule with around seven grams of ash from your cremation, pack it into a small canister and then fly it into space. You can select different options for your final resting place: Earth's orbit, the Moon or deep space. All packages include a flight capsule imprinted with a personal message, invitations to friends and relatives to attend the launch, a group memorial service before blastoff and a video of proceedings. If you are interested and want more information, just visit www.celestis.com.

🔮 Why do old movies always seem so jerky and speeded up?

🔬 Authorities estimate that 80 per cent of early pre-talkie movies have been lost forever. And of those that survive, many seem bizarrely speeded up.

According to the silent movie appreciation society "The Silent Majority", we are not seeing old films in the way they would have been viewed by their original audiences. Since the coming of sound, cine-film has run at a standard speed of 24 frames per second. Back around the turn of the century, rates varied from 16–18 frames per second, so when played on an unadjusted projector today, films dating from that era run too fast. Physical damage to film stock over time, such as broken sprocket holes, can also cause jerky images.

However, sometimes the speeded-up effect is intentional. Comedy directors often "undercranked" their cameras to create scenes of amusing, frenetic activity.

where did the term catch-22 come from?

The catch in question is the title and main plot device of Joseph Heller's first novel, a satire of military bureaucracy set in World War II. Essentially, any soldier in Heller's American Air Force could go home if they were insane. All they had to do was ask. But as soon as they asked, they would be declared sane because they had shown rational concern for their own safety. When told this, the hero, Yossarian, whistles: "That's some catch, that Catch 22." To which the corps' doctor replies: "It's the best there is."

The phrase soon became shorthand for a situation where, whichever alternative you select, you can't win. Mathematicians have even devised rules for working out the cause of Catch-22 situations, and what to do when confronted with them.

The reason Heller picked 22 as the number emerged in an interview he gave some months before his death in December 1999. He explained that his original title was *Catch-18*, but just before the book appeared, his publisher told him that another book had come out, called *Mila 18*. Compelled to come up with another number, Heller simply decided on 22 – and the rest is literary history.

who invented the scottish bagpipes, and how do they work?

While the origin of the bagpipes is still disputed – not least by the Scots – the basic idea certainly didn't come from Scotland. References to a reed instrument powered by air squeezed from a bag first appeared in European manuscripts during the ninth century, and some historians think the instrument may date back to the Romans.

The modern Highland bagpipes use four pipes to make their music: the "chanter", which has finger-holes for playing the melody, and three "drones", playing single, continuous notes in the tenor and bass ranges. All four pipes are powered by air squeezed out of a bag held under the player's arm.

The unique sound made by the bagpipes bears witness to their great antiquity: all four pipes are mutually tuned according to an ancient musical scale that is no longer used in European music. Whatever one thinks of the sound, it is one that has struck terror into the hearts of enemy soldiers for centuries.

The Pope is the head of the Catholic church, but who is the leader of Islam?

Unlike the Roman Catholic church, there is no one particular individual at the head of the Islamic faith. Islam allows and expects every member to interpret the Koran in their own way. Muslim countries tend to be spiritually guided by their own political or religious leaders.

Some sects, such as the Ismaelis from Iran, look to the Aga Khan, whom they regard as the current descendant of the Prophet Allah. The more widespread Shi'ites used to have just two or three wise elders, but since the fall of the Shah of Iran they have adopted a system of "local" leadership, with many mullahs to provide guidance and interpretation of the Koran.

Sunni Moslems – the largest Muslim sect, mainly based in Saudi Arabia and Egypt – used to look to the Caliph. But since the end of the Caliphat in the early nineteenth century, the King of Saudi Arabia and the Egyptian Premier have both claimed to be the leader of the faith.

technology
and
engineering

🌀 why do clocks go clockwise?

🅰 Because that's the way the shadow on a sundial moves. Invented by the early Egyptians around 3,500BC, the first sundial was in the form of a stick in the ground. Being in the Northern Hemisphere, the Egyptians saw that the sun was due south at noon, and thus cast a shadow due north. As the sun continued on its westward journey across the skies, the shadow moved eastward thus performing what we now call "clockwise" movement.

If sundials had been invented in the Southern Hemisphere, where the sun is always to the north, clockwise would have been in the opposite direction. At noon, the shadow would point due south, but still move eastwards as the day drew on. A sundial designed for London will work in Australia, but the numbers run counter-clockwise.

🌀 How do quartz watches work?

🅰 Through what's called the piezo-electric effect. If you squeeze certain types of crystal, including quartz, they generate an electric field (that's also how those kitchen gas-lighters create their spark). The same effect also works in reverse: apply an electric field to quartz, and it will change shape. If you apply an alternating voltage fast enough, you can persuade a suitably-cut quartz crystal to vibrate at four different "natural frequencies" of anything from 32,768 to 4,100,000 times per second.

In a quartz watch or clock, these vibrations form the "tick-tock" signals needed to mark out time. Count 32,768 of them and you've got a second (by comparison, mechanical clocks manage no more than around 5 "tick-tocks" a second). The faster the vibration, the more accurate the time-keeping: a cheap quartz watch will easily manage to keep time to within one second a month, and a precise quartz clock can keep time to around 1 second a decade.

🔲 Did Baird really invent the TV?

🔳 Well, yes and no. Scottish engineer John Logie Baird certainly demonstrated the first working TV system in 1924 – and followed it up in 1928 with colour TV pictures. But the system he developed isn't anything like the one we use today. Baird used a mechanical approach, a rotating disc invented in 1884 by Paul Nipkow, who had developed the principles of television scanning.

Others favoured electronic approaches. In 1897, Karl Ferdinand Braun succeeded in producing narrow electron streams from cathode-ray tubes (CRT) that could trace patterns on fluorescent screens. Ten years later, the Russian scientist Boris Rosing suggested using a CRT as a TV receiver and produced crude geometrical patterns on a fluorescent screen. So, by the early part of the last century the basics of today's TV system had already been identified.

During the 1920s, the émigré Russian electrical engineer Vladimir Zworykin worked on cathode ray tube systems for TV, and in 1932 the Radio Corporation of America (RCA) incorporated his work into the first all-electronic TV. By the early 1950s, all-electronic colour TVs had been developed which could still display black and white pictures. This basic cathode-ray technology has since become ubiquitous and can be found in living rooms the world over, while Baird's system has become a museum piece.

🔲 How do you curve glass for windscreens?

🔳 Glass can't be bent like metals can because it is brittle. But when heated, it becomes more plastic and much more amenable to being curved. During "sag bending", a sheet of glass is supported around its edges and the middle heated to 600°C. As the glass softens, it begins to sag under its own weight. A die is then used to press the final touches in the heated glass for intricate shaping.

There is, however, a limit to how far a sheet of glass can be bent

Technology and engineering

while remaining transparent. Overdo it and the glass will wrinkle – not what you want in a car windscreen. Glass destined for use in cars is also toughened, usually by sandwiching plastic layers between sheets of glass before the whole thing is heated and shaped. Even if it becomes shattered, this laminated glass does not break up into razor-sharp splinters.

💬 why, when silicon chips have changed so much, have PCBs stayed the same?

💬 Silicon chip production has changed radically since early days, but the printed circuit boards (PCBs) that connect them together are still made in much the same way.

However, Dr Andrew Shipway, a surface chemist at the Hebrew University in Jerusalem, has come up with a process that could make it possible to download circuits from paper. "I became interested in making circuits on the nanoscale," says Dr Shipway, who specialises in nanotechnology, "and I took some of the technology from that field."

Shipway says the process is the opposite of how circuits have always been made. "Usually something is made on the macroscale first," he explains, "then it is scaled down. What we've done here is to start on the nanoscale and work up."

The standard way of making circuit boards has been to "take a slab of copper," as he puts it, and etch away bits to create the required component. But he has reversed this "top-down" approach and developed a "bottom-up" approach, starting with nothing and adding only the necessary features.

Shipway plays down suggestions that the technique could be used to cheaply produce items such as mobile phones, as the paper circuits would have to be used in conjunction with other components. "Downloading a complete device is a long way away," he says.

🤖 How do slot machines detect counterfeit coins?

🤖 Slot machines run everything that's put into them through a rigorous series of checks before letting you play. Precisely how they do this varies, but most begin by checking the coin for width, diameter, solidity, weight and metallic composition. The first of these checks is the simplest, as the size of the entry slot prevents people from putting in anything that's wider or greater in diameter than the slot itself. After a coin is passed through the slot, it is sometimes tested for solidity: the centre is probed to make sure it isn't a washer or one of those foreign coins with a hole in the middle.

If the coin gets past the probe, it will then fall onto a pivoting cradle. If it's too light, it fails to tip the cradle and falls into the reject channel: if it matches the expected weight, it's tipped onto the runway. Rolling on, the coin passes magnets that check what it is made from. If metals of the wrong magnetic properties are detected, the coin will be pulled off course and flipped into the reject channel. However, if your coin is made of the right stuff, it will be accepted and you'll get your train ticket, soft drink or nudges.

🤖 Why are the numbers on calculators and computers arranged differently from those on a telephone?

🤖 On key telephones, the digits run from top to bottom, while on computer and electronic calculator keypads it is the other way round. Computer and calculator keypads evolved directly from the old mechanical calculators, which for reasons involving cogs and levers had to be constructed with the "9" placed on top. The layout was not changed – the product was simply not considered a serious enough tool for its ergonomics to matter.

The keyphone, however, was a new invention and endured many hundreds of tests of its ergonomics to make it faster and more accurate to use. When trials began in 1962 the numbers were arranged in two rows of five, progressing in 1967 to three rows of three with zero at the bottom. After more years and yet more trials the keyphone became generally available in 1976. With the advent of electronic switchboards, the star and hash keys were added, producing the modern keypad.

While we're on the subject of keypads – that little "bobble" on the 5 is to help blind people make phone-calls, by allowing them to know where their finger is in relation to the other numbers – that is, 2 is just above it, 9 is to the lower right.

How does "stealth" technology work?

First used in action during the US invasion of Panama in December 1989, the F-117A Nighthawk stealth aircraft is the most futuristic-looking machine in service today. But that sci-fi shape plays a key role in its ability to keep a low profile on enemy radar.

Ordinary aircraft simply bounce back much of the radio-wave energy that hits them when they are struck by a radar beam, thus giving the enemy a nice, big signal to lock on to. But the angular shape of the F-117A's fuselage means that radar beams do not bounce back directly, but are scattered all over the sky, fuzzing out its radar image. The Nighthawk is also coated with a thick coat of black carbon fibres, which mop up a lot of the radar energy and transform it into heat. Even the cockpit canopy is coated with transparent, radar-absorbing indium-tin-oxide, which prevents the pilot's helmet from bouncing back any telltale signals. The result is an aircraft that produces a radar image about the size of a small bird – hundreds of times smaller than a conventional plane of similar size.

Planes aren't the only vehicles to benefit from the stealth treatment, though. The US Navy has developed a stealthy ship, and the British Army's new tank – the Advanced Composite Armoured Vehicle Platform (ACAVP) – is made of a plastic and glass fibre composite making it much less visible to radar than its predecessors. It is also much lighter, weighing in at just 28 tons, compared to the 68-ton Challenger II tank. In the Bosnian conflict, normal tanks were too heavy to negotiate many bridges.

That said, a plastic tank does have its drawbacks. Although the ACAVP can withstand medium-calibre ammunition, a high-velocity tank shell will stop it in its tracks. The tank's improved power-to-weight ratio, however, will get it out of trouble faster than a Challenger II. And if it is hit, the plastic shell of its bodywork will buckle rather than disintegrate into lethal shrapnel.

⚙ Does cold fusion really work?

🅰 In March 1989 Martin Fleischmann of Southampton University and his American colleague Stanley Pons claimed to have solved the world's energy problems using nothing more than a jar of heavy water and some platinum electrodes. Many scientists dismissed the claim as ludicrous, and when others failed to repeat the results, "cold fusion" fell into disrepute.

One of the key criticisms of the claim was that, if the two researchers really had triggered fusion in a jam-jar, it would have generated huge amounts of neutron particles – and killed them before they could tell anyone about their breakthrough. Very few scientists still believe that Fleischmann and Pons really did create fusion: most think that the pair probably made errors when trying to account for all the energy going in and coming out of their system, fooling them into thinking they'd made a net gain in energy output. Even so, the claims have never gone away, and Japanese corporations are reported to be still taking the idea seriously.

The German engineering genius behind the Apollo space programme: Wernher von Braun. On 8 September 1944, he and his colleagues unleashed the first-ever ballistic missiles from their launch site in the Netherlands. Called V-2s, they quickly reached their maximum speed of more than 5,000km/hr, and after a few minutes they had reached their targets – and their one-ton warheads blasted the suburbs of Paris and London.

It was a terrifyingly impressive achievement – but the fact is that the V-2 was a triumph of overwhelming ambition over military effectiveness. Over the next seven months, a total of around 3,200 V-2 rockets were launched; around 1,300 against targets in England, with a similar number unleashed against the Belgian port of Antwerp alone. Yet, despite this bombardment, the final death toll from V-2s was only about 5,000 – appalling, of course, but by the cold reckoning of military planning, a hopelessly inadequate strike-rate of fewer than two deaths per missile.

In economic terms, the V-2 made even less sense. Experts estimate that each rocket cost the equivalent of half-a-dozen fighter aircraft to build, with the V-2 programme having an effect on Nazi military spending equivalent to that of the Allied atomic bomb project.

As the American V-2 historian Michael Neufeld says, "German missile development shortened the war, just as its advocates said it would – but in the favour of the Allies". In the end, not even von Braun's genius could get around the sheer inefficiency of the rockets, which demand huge boosters to launch even tiny warheads – thus needing to be aimed with a precision that was far beyond the V-2's capabilities.

However, the bitterest irony of the V-2, unique in military history, is that more people died in the manufacturing process – mostly forced Czech labour – than were killed when the weapon was actually deployed against Allied civilian targets.

where is the safest place to sit on a commercial airliner?

Britain's Civil Aviation Authority and Transport Ministry has no official answer to this question. But according to one publicity-shy RAF officer, the black box flight recorder is placed in the back of the plane because "that's always the least damaged part of the wreckage. Draw your own conclusions."

More important than your seat number is the direction you're facing. In RAF troop transport planes, all seats face toward the tail – i.e. backwards. According to Group Captain David Reader, from the RAF's Aviation Medicine Centre, the RAF decided to fix all seats backwards 30 years ago, after accident research proved that it saved lives. Passengers seated backwards have a larger surface area of their body cushioned and are less likely to suffer serious injury when they're forced into the chair than they would be out of it.

So, to survive a plane crash, the best advice is to sit facing backwards, at the rear of the plane, against the toughest bulkhead you can find.

who invented the electric guitar, and when was it produced?

The very first guitar with electronic pick-ups was invented by Adolf Rickenbacker in 1932, based on a Hawaiian guitar with seven strings, that was played in your lap. Its round body and long neck earned it the nickname "the frying pan".

Leo Fender is credited with inventing the first "solid body" commercial instrument around 50 years ago, going on to create the legendary Fender Telecaster and Stratocaster. Orville Gibson – whose big acoustic jazz guitars had featured electronic pick-ups before Fender appeared on the scene – fought back when master guitarist Les Paul designed a solid electric guitar for him based around a chunk of wooden railway sleeper. Paul also went on to invent multi-track recording.

Today, all three designs – the Rickenbacker, the Fender and the Gibson – remain virtually unchanged. Production models of these classics are nothing like the most expensive guitars on the market, but they are still the instruments everyone wants to own.

what's the best way of dealing with nuclear waste?

When nuclear power first took off, governments did not worry too much about what to do with the waste. They were more interested in getting hold of enough plutonium to make their own arsenals of nuclear weapons. They do worry now, though – yet despite years of intensive research, the best solution that anyone has come up with is to bury it deep underground.

The problem is that the tonnes of waste must be kept safe for tens of thousands of years – and no one knows what might happen over that period. Water may seep in, polluting drinking supplies, while a new ice age could totally destroy almost any site. Firing it off into space isn't a good idea either – rockets aren't totally reliable, and you wouldn't want tonnes of nuclear waste pouring down on your head.

How disposable are disposable cameras?

When it first came out, the disposable camera was an incredible success – and one of the most wasteful consumer products ever. Following its launch by Fuji in 1989, Kodak, Konica and Agfa all jumped on the bandwagon, marketing their cameras as "single use". Yet, with the original models, even if all 24 frames were fired using flash, the battery inside the camera still had 90 per cent of its power left. Once the film was taken out by the processing lab, the rest of the camera (including the battery) was simply discarded, often ending up in a local landfill site.

As environmental issues came to the fore in the 1990s, the film companies realised the error of their ways – and single-use cameras are now a recycling success story, About three million are sold in the UK each year, and in 1999 Kodak collected over two million units from processing labs across the country. Most of the cameras are sent back to their country of origin – China – to be reloaded with film and repackaged for resale.

Depending on their condition when they reach China, some can be re-used up to five times. If a camera cannot be re-used, then its parts are broken down and recycled. New designs make removing the battery a much easier task and consumers seem to have grasped the idea that – in the form of an almost fresh AA alkaline battery – they can get something back for their money.

why is cheese traditionally cut with a wire, not a knife?

A knife is an incredibly powerful force-to-pressure converter, amplifying the force applied by hand and arm into a very high pressure. The sharper the knife, the higher the amplification – because the edge concentrates the force into a smaller area, boosting the cutting pressure. A decent knife is easily capable of generating well over a tonne of force per square inch along its fine edge – simple but very efficient.

However, cheese is sticky and the broad sides of the blade give it plenty to grab on to as the knife cuts through. A wire can be as thin as a knife-edge – with good cutting pressure – but has far less surface area, allowing it to pass easily through cheese.

How do computer viruses work?

A true computer virus is a set of instructions that "infects" other computer programs, altering them to include a version of itself. Like a biological virus, which has no reproductive system of its own and "borrows" those of organisms it infects to reproduce, a computer virus uses the host machine's normal processes (like starting up and loading programs) to spread itself.

When most people talk about viruses they mean any program that gets into a computer "unmasked" and causes damage. In fact, viruses are only one among many such programs, which are known to computer security experts as "Trojan Horses". This type of program is disguised as something useful or interesting but subsequently proves to be less beneficial than expected.

A Trojan Horse can be any program the unsuspecting victim loads onto his or her computer, which can cause mayhem by making it crash, wiping out data or slowing it down. A well-written virus will scan a computer looking for healthy programs to infect, and then makes copies of itself. These copies, in turn, look for more programs to infect and make copies of themselves, and so on and on and on …

🔾 why do people create computer viruses?

🔾 It's a common myth that all virus writers are spotty teen hackers with a grudge against society. Virus writers are as likely to be computer professionals as adolescents. The first viruses were experiments created by computer researchers to study code which could "build itself".

Few viruses are written for personal gain. There's not much in the way of fame or glory. An exception – although not strictly a virus was – the AIDS Trojan Horse program. In 1989, 10,000 copies of an AIDS information pack were mailed out by a company calling itself PC Cyborg. The pack had a disk with a program on it that hid itself on the user's hard disk and, on the 90th boot-up, encrypted the entire hard disk, making the machine inaccessible to the user. A message flashed up on the screen demanding money in return for the encryption key. After an international hunt, the culprits were tracked down to Panama.

How close are we to creating a hydrogen fuel car?

People have been talking about hydrogen fuel cars for ages, but now they may be just a few years away. The fuel cell used to power such a car consists of two electrodes bathed in an electrolyte solution. Hydrogen is pumped in through a pipe attached to the negative electrode (anode) and oxygen via the positive electrode (cathode). At the anode, hydrogen atoms are split into protons and electrons. The protons then pass through the electrolyte and react with the oxygen at the cathode, while the electrons flow through an external circuit. The resulting electrical current may be used to propel vehicles.

Fuel cell powered cars are already starting to emerge in prototype form – and they can't come fast enough. As fuel cells produce only water as a waste product, they're far cleaner than petrol engines, and more fuel-efficient. The biggest drawback is the need for regular hydrogen stations, to replace today's petrol stations. This is chiefly a logistics problem.

Despite its fearsomely explosive image – often mistakenly used to explain those pictures of the Hindenburg airship disaster, which was actually due to inflammable paint – hydrogen is safer than petrol.

What's the most ferocious fire encountered by firefighters?

According to Chris Goodison, head of human factors at the UK's Fire Research and Development Group, the heat produced by sudden explosions, such as flash-overs and backdraughts, is the most intense. In these events, firefighting clothing that is made from heat-resistant fibres such as Nomex has to withstand temperatures of 500–600 °C.

❓ How do depleted uranium shells work?

For armour-piercing shells, you want to pack a big punch into a small volume travelling at high speed. With a density of 19 tonnes per cubic metre – almost double that of lead – uranium can pack a lot of mass into a very small volume. Even a 120mm round can contain approximately 10lb (4.5kg) of solid DU. When it hits a tank, the aluminium cartridge casing rips off and the DU "penetrator" in the nose rockets through armour and splits into melting fragments at a temperature of 5,000°C. There is no explosive in the round, but its mass and speed are enough to lift a 30-ton tank one foot in the air.

Called the "silver bullet" by tank commanders, DU rounds are the most effective way of stopping tanks. The British, French and Americans all use DU-tipped rounds, with the Americans using it as armour for their M1 tanks, as well as in munitions. The most devastating modern use of DU was by the A-10 "tankbuster" aircraft (nicknamed the Warthog) during in the Gulf War. Armed with a seven-barrelled rotary cannon, it fires 30mm armour-piercing DU bullets at the rate of 4,200 per minute.

Concern about the health effects of DU have led to growing use of tungsten instead of DU – a metal that is slightly denser even than DU, but more expensive.

❓ Is there any value in old electronic components?

You bet there is. Cellphones and other electronic gadgets contain gold, silver and copper, and millions of them are being broken up so that the metal can be extracted. One tonne of chips can produce around 150g of pure gold, and a Japanese manufacturer is planning to use magnesium instead of plastic for phone casings, as it makes them much easier to recycle.

Using the bottle-bank idea, mobile-phone companies in the UK have set up 400 collection bins at sites around the country, into which you can drop your old phones.

How are cranes erected on building sites?

We've all seen cranes that appear as if from nowhere on city building sites far smaller than the crane itself. Often called "climbing tower" cranes, their name holds the secret to their miraculous ability to sprout from nowhere. A small mobile crane builds the first few mast sections (the latticed steel superstructure) and adds a climbing frame slightly larger than a standard section of the mast. The operator's cab, the jib and counter-weight are then placed on the top. The climbing frame, which is three-sided (or with a fourth, detachable side), incorporates hydraulic rams that lift the cab and jib structure, leaving room for another modular section of the mast. This is added by the crane itself – say, by being swung into position via a trolley system, into the fourth side. This is then bolted to the section below by workers on the climbing frame. The whole process is repeated, adding sections until the crane reaches the required height. It can take up to a day to fit three sections.

Why did the "unsinkable" Titanic sink?

While everyone knows the *Titanic* hit an iceberg, the design of the giant ship was supposed to keep her afloat no matter what. Her structure was divided into watertight sections, and up to four of the sections could supposedly be flooded without sinking the ship. But, as the crew and passengers discovered on the night of April 14 1912, the *Titanic*'s watertight compartments weren't watertight: there was a gap at the top of the bulkheads, which allowed water to slop over from one to the next, eventually triggering a catastrophic tilt and sinking the ship.

The sheer size of the hole made by the iceberg – around 300ft long – didn't help either. New studies have suggested the size of the hole was partly caused by the hull suffering "brittle fracture" in the cold North Atlantic. In a report presented to the Society of Naval Architects and Marine Engineers in 1993, the naval architect William Garzke claimed that the metal used to build the ship was particularly high in sulphur, which becomes brittle in extreme cold. A fire in a coalbunker, combined with sub-freezing water outside, increased stress on the hull.

Garzke and Dana Yoeger, from the Woods Hole Oceanographic Institution (which found the wreck in 1986), suggest that glancing blows from the iceberg popped rivets and broke the ship's metal seams. To test the theory, a small chunk of hull steel was retrieved from the *Titanic* in 1995 and placed with a piece of modern ship steel in an alcohol bath cooled to the temperature of the sea on the night of the disaster. A 67lb (31kg) pendulum was then swung against both pieces. The modern metal was bent into a V-shape but the *Titanic* metal snapped in half.

According to Garzke, it was a finding with tragic implications. He estimates that without the brittle fracture tendency, the *Titanic* might have lasted a couple of hours longer, and the nearest ship, the *Carpathia*, may have got there in time to rescue some of the 1,500 passengers who perished.

why are ınternet calls to anywhere in the world so cheap?

One of the best things about the Internet is that sending e-mail or surfing for information costs the same amount wherever you are. No matter how far away you are from the destination, it never costs more than the price of a local call.

If you phone your friend in California, you are making a long-distance call and are charged accordingly. If, however, you e-mail them or visit their website, you are not actually phoning California at all – you are making a local call to your Internet Service Provider (ISP).

So what happens to the long-distance bit? That part of the call is made by the ISP, who absorb the cost. Prices can be kept low because the ISPs lease telecommunication lines that span the world, linking up the tens of millions of computers on the Internet. The bandwidth is huge, so the lines can handle a vast number of calls (problems are usually due to routing technology).

The ISP-leased lines are relatively cheap to run, and are open 24-hours-a-day, 365-days-a-year. Maintenance costs are pretty low, so advertising and subscriptions are more than enough to pay for this world-wide network – and still ensure a healthy profit for ISPs.

who invented the telescope?

The basic optical principles were first described by the English scientist Roger Bacon in the thirteenth century, although according to the textbooks, it wasn't until 1608 that the Dutchman Hans Lippershey mounted lenses in a tube and turned them into the first refracting telescope. But in 1992, the late astronomer and historian Colin Ronan claimed that Lippershey had been pipped to the post by two English scientists, Leonard and Thomas Digges, thirty years earlier. According to Ronan, the Digges telescope was intended for use by the military, and all references to it were banned by the Elizabethan equivalent of the Official Secrets Act.

Whatever the truth, Galileo improved the basic design of the telescope to make pioneering observations of the Moon and Jupiter. And in 1663, the Scottish astronomer James Gregory conceived the reflecting telescope, which used a curved mirror to bring light rays to a focus rather than bending them. This rid telescopic images of nasty false colours caused by refraction in the glass lens. Sir Isaac Newton was the first person to actually build a reflecting telescope, in 1688.

As well as giving better images, the reflecting telescope could also be used to study far fainter objects, as it's easier to make a huge mirror than a huge lens.

🔹 who invented plastic?

🔹 The credit for inventing the very first plastic is usually given to the American inventor John Hyatt, who in 1869 patented Celluloid, an easily-mouldable material that could serve as a substitute for ivory in the manufacture of billiard balls.

Made from a mixture of nitro-cellulose, alcohol, ether and camphor, Celluloid proved surprisingly versatile, becoming the basis for photographic film, shirt collars and products such as baby rattles. Its biggest failing, however, was its poor response to heat, which would make it burst into flames. It took another 40 years for the first "thermosetting" plastic to emerge. Called Bakelite, it made a fortune for its inventor, the Belgian-American chemist Leo Baekeland.

🔹 can radio waves affect computers?

🔹 It depends on how old your computer is. We've all heard of how a radio can go fuzzy thanks to a food mixer in the next room. This is due to a phenomenon known as electromagnetic interference (EMI). All electronic circuits emit some electromagnetic waves and may cause interference in other instruments under the right circumstances. That's why you are not allowed to use mobile phones or laptop computers on a plane during take-off; stray waves could bounce off the wings and into the cockpit.

It was once feared we would all end up in a jungle of electromagnetic waves, as use of computers and mobile phones spread. Europe, therefore, introduced the electromagnetic compatibility directive. This became UK law on 1 January 1996, and requires that all new electronic goods emit a minimum of interference and are fully capable of withstanding bursts of EMI.

🔵 Are Furbies artificially intelligent?

🔴 Furbies are among the biggest hit toys of recent years – more than five million of these chatty electronic creatures have been sold so far. With their big eyes and silly voices, Furbies are certainly pesky. But, if the publicity about them is to be believed, they are also highly sophisticated. Each Furby is said to possess artificial intelligence, allowing it to learn about its human owners and respond to them.

Furbies begin by talking nonsense called "Furbish", which gradually turns to English. But sceptics insist this doesn't mean Furbies are learning: they could be using just a simple memory chip that releases progressively more impressive sentences over time.

Either way, Furbies highlight a key issue in the quest for artificial intelligence – how can you tell if a machine possesses it? In 1950, the British mathematical genius Alan Turing came up with what is now called the Turing Test; if you can't tell the difference between how the machine responds and how a human would in the same circumstances, then the machine is "thinking". It's a test that cleverly puts the question back in the lap (or rather mind) of each individual. So, while a five-year-old might think a Furby passes the Turing Test, few adults would be fooled. Well, not for more than five minutes, anyhow.

🔵 Is it possible to control the weather?

🔴 In the 1940s and 1950s, many studies were carried out into the possibility of ending droughts by "seeding" clouds with particles of silver iodide or "dry ice" – solid carbon dioxide. The idea was that water molecules would cluster around these substances and fall to the ground as sizeable droplets of rain. So much for the theory – the practice has produced mixed results and cloud seeding doesn't seem very reliable.

technology and engineering

In the late 1940s, the American chemist and Nobel Prize winner Irving Langmuir suggested an even more outlandish idea – that hurricanes could be tamed by chemicals. While they are incredibly powerful – releasing more energy in a single day than the US electric grid delivers in a year – hurricanes are formed by energy cycles that could be vulnerable to disruption.

In 1947, Langmuir put his ideas to the test, flying above a tropical storm and dumping around 100kg of dry ice into it. Analysing the evolution of the storm, Langmuir insisted that it had changed track after the dry ice had been dropped into it. Sceptics dismissed his claim as a mere coincidence, arguing that it was inconceivable that so little dry ice could have affected something so vast and powerful as a hurricane. Even so, similar experiments carried out in the late 1960s suggested that hurricanes could be made significantly weaker by using silver iodide to trigger rainfall in order to tame vicious winds.

why do some car headlights have a bluish tint?

Known in the trade as gas discharge lights, these bluish lights are actually a big improvement on conventional car headlights. Instead of the standard light bulb-like filament, gas discharge lights are filled with an inert gas, xenon, which gives out light when exposed to a voltage. The light is both more intense – producing about three times as much light as conventional headlights – and closer in colour to the blue-white brilliance of daylight.

According to Graham Fudge of Vauxhall Cars (UK), discharge lights once took a few seconds to reach full intensity, but now they work as soon as they're switched on. As a result, we can expect to see more cars being fitted with "xenons" in the years to come, which is good news for road safety.

How do metal detectors work?

Common treasure-hunt metal detectors work by simultaneously inducing and detecting magnetic fields in metal objects buried in the ground.

The business end of a detector consists of two concentric circular coils. Alternating electric (AC) current flows through the outer "transmitter" coil, producing a perpendicular magnetic field, as in an electric motor. As the AC reverses direction, thousands of times per second, the magnetic field also alternates, projecting into the ground as a series of magnetic "pulses".

These pulses induce secondary, weaker magnetic fields in magnetically conductive buried objects, such as gold coins or drink can tabs. The inner "receiver" coil registers these induced fields in the form of electric currents, which flow into the detector's control box for analysis.

By relating field frequencies to different metals, and field strengths to different depths under ground, the treasure-hunter can judge when to switch from a hi-tech detector to low-tech shovel.

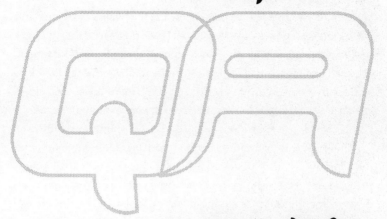

Health,
medicine
and
Nutrition

Does vitamin c really improve your health?

Linus Pauling, the greatest chemist of the twentieth century and still the only scientist to win two Nobel Peace prizes, certainly thought so. From the late 1960s onwards, he took 3-gram doses of vitamin C every day (50 times the current recommendation), and in 1970 was sufficiently impressed by the effects to bring out a book – *Vitamin C and the Common Cold* – in which he recommended taking one to four grams each day to keep colds at bay and enjoy optimum health.

The book was an instant success and triggered a huge demand for vitamin C. It also provoked a storm of protest from the medical profession, with the US Food and Drug Administration denouncing the claim as having no scientific basis.

Today, the medical profession is more receptive to Pauling's claims, though still with reservations. Scientists concede that vitamin C combats so-called free radicals – highly reactive substances that can trigger cancer and heart disease. But whether large doses can actually prevent such illnesses is far from clear.

A major study published in 2000 suggests that taking one gram of vitamin C each day will not guarantee protection against colds, but can make them less severe and long-lasting. To which Pauling would no doubt have said: "well, take bigger doses then." It doesn't seem to have done him much harm at any rate: he lived until the ripe old age of 93.

Is genetically modified food really necessary?

The debate over genetically modified (GM) foods has intensified over the past few years. According to the supermarkets, consumers do not want GM foods, or GM ingredients in their food. Major companies are already instructing their suppliers that they do not want milk or meat from animals that may have been fed on GM ingredients. But the biotechnology companies argue that GM crops will be cheaper to produce, because fewer pesticides and herbicides will need to be used.

On a global scale, supporters of GM say it will be the only way to sustainably feed the world – not simply because more crops will survive to harvest, but because GM can allow food to grow in drought conditions or saline soils. However, the real problem with world food supply isn't a simple lack of food, but that there's not enough of it in places that really need it, and too much of it where it's not needed – like inside obese Europeans and Americans.

what alternatives are there to GM?

Scientists in China have come up with their own alternative to genetically modified crops – enormous vegetables grown from seeds that have been to outer space. Guangzhou City Greenhome Technology Development Company is one of six institutions in China dedicated to growing seeds that have made the trip. Its greenhouses are filled with two-metre long melons and oversized chilli peppers, while the company brochures promise carrots that grow to more than a metre in length and tomatoes that weigh a kilogram or two.

Chinese farmers, who often find it difficult to produce high quality crops, are welcoming the horticultural giants. The vegetables are also reported to have superior nutritional value. Laboratory trials indicate that they contain double the vitamins, 7 per cent more iron and 25 per cent more trace elements than their terrestrial rivals. The Chinese suggest that changes to the seeds, which are sent into space for 15 days, are caused by the lack of oxygen, zero gravity and being bombarded by cosmic rays.

However, while these conditions can affect DNA, causing genetic mutations, British biotechnology scientists remain sceptical. It may turn out that the mutations in the Chinese crops are just flukes, or that the vegetables were inflated by a quirk in the growing process, in a similar way to the prize-winning marrows at your local fête.

Q: is there any easy way to tell organic food apart from GM or non-organic types?

A: No – not with complete certainty, anyhow. In principle, to test for genetic modification, one simply picks out the added or engineered genes in the modified variety using a chemical DNA probe. The trouble is, the shorter the gene sequence, the less accurate this test becomes. So tests work better with raw materials than with ready-made processed foods such as sauces and pizzas, where the DNA gets fragmented during the processing (which, incidentally, is also what happens in your stomach when you eat the stuff).

The other drawback is that although chemical DNA probe tests are very sensitive – because they work by amplifying the gene sequence – they do have a lower limit beyond which the modified DNA cannot be detected. If the total DNA in the food has been altered by only a tiny amount, the test may not pick up on it. So you can't be absolutely sure that food is GM-free, except by tracing it back to its original source.

As for organic foods, there is no lab-based test that can distinguish the organic from the non-organic. This is because there is a whole system involved in organic food production and there are just too many different factors to test for (some of which probably couldn't be measured anyway). Instead you should look for a reputable label, such as the symbol of the Soil Association, which certifies organic products. Such labels are your best guarantee of genuinely organic food.

Q: Are sperm counts really going down?

A: In 1992, Dr Niels Skakkebaek of the University of Copenhagen caused a sensation by claiming that sperm counts had been declining since the 1930s. The claim led to fears that hormone-like chemicals in water and food packaging were to blame. But later reports suggested that sperm counts actually rose by 15 per cent between 1970 and 1994 – in America at least. As yet, no-one is sure which research is more reliable, although early indications suggest that reports of a decline are less likely to be correct.

what defines a psychopath?

Despite their reputation as mad axemen, psychopaths are far more insidious members of our community. With their ruthlessness, impulsiveness and chilling lack of remorse, psychopaths can be found throughout society, from schoolyard bully to despotic dictator.

It's estimated that around 3 per cent of the world population might show signs of the condition. Yet the cause of psychopathy – or "antisocial personality disorder" – remains a mystery. There is some evidence that the brains of psychopaths have failed to mature emotionally, and hints that poor bonding between mother and child may be involved. It is more likely, however, that there is no single cause for this most disturbing of personality traits – and perhaps no cure, either.

what are blood groups, and what happens if you're given the wrong sort?

Blood groups are decided by the type of so-called antigen protein – A, B or neither ("O") – sitting on the surface of your red blood cells. What type you've got is determined by genetics, so you can't belong to a blood group different from that of both your parents. So, for example, if dad is O and mum is A, their kids can only belong to O and A.

The principal blood groups are A, B, AB and O, and their relative frequency varies across the world. For example, while O is most common in the UK and north-west Europe, A is more common in Scandinavia, and B in central Asia.

Because it lacks either the A or B-type antigens, O-type blood can be given to anyone. Similarly, because they've got both antigens on their blood cells, people belonging to the AB group can be given any type of blood. But giving, say, A-type blood to B-type patients can be disastrous. In 1900, the German pathologist Karl Landsteiner, who pioneered the study of different blood groups, discovered that red blood cells will agglutinate (clump together) when they come into contact with blood from people from different groups.

After Landsteiner, other researchers discovered a whole range of other antigens; such as the Rhesus antigen system in 1940. Since then about 400 new antigens have been discovered.

How do general anaesthetics work?

Amazingly, 150 years after they were first used, the miraculous ability of anaesthetics to kill pain is still not fully understood. As a result, patients are still occasionally being killed by overdoses, or suffering the trauma of being paralysed during operations while still able to feel pain.

Scientists used to think that anaesthetics worked by somehow dissolving into the walls of nerve cells, preventing them transmitting pain. But growing evidence suggests that anaesthetics home in on very specific proteins on the surface of nerve cells. Solving this mystery could speed the development of safer anaesthetics – and put an end to all the horror stories.

Are there parts of the body you can operate on without anaesthetic?

The reason you feel pain more acutely in some parts of your body is because of different concentrations of sensory nerve cells: the more closely packed they are, the more chance there is of even small amounts of damage being detected by them. This is why it is possible to cut parts of your body with a scalpel and not feel a thing – while damage with a blunter instrument would be agonising.

The way that nerves are arranged is also important, which is why cutting the intestines doesn't hurt, although stretching or contracting them does – as people with bowel disease know only too well. Amazingly enough, you don't need any anaesthetic to operate on the brain, as it doesn't contain any pain sensors. Surgeons give a local anaesthetic simply because they have to cut through the skull to get at it. Once in there, they can rummage about with their patients fully conscious and not feeling a thing.

🔘 what is gulf war syndrome?

🔘 Many of those people who fought against Iraq in 1990–1 subsequently complained of suffering from "Gulf War Syndrome". Soldiers got debilitating illnesses such as chronic fatigue, rashes, muscle pain, headaches, respiratory and gastrointestinal problems. The Pentagon has since admitted that more than 20,000 US troops may have been affected when Allied forces bombed Iraqi chemical weapons installations. Scientists from King's College, London, have also suggested that the multiple vaccinations given to protect soldiers from biological weapons could have caused the illness.

As many as 5,000 British Gulf War veterans are thought to be suffering from various conditions related to their service in the Gulf and 500 may have died from these conditions. The lasting impact on Iraqis may be more deadly. After the War, hundreds of Iraqi babies were born with appalling disfigurements, which many scientists claim is the result of their fathers – Iraqi soldiers – being exposed to some of the 900,000 US Army rounds and shells tipped with depleted uranium (Britain fired just 88 similar rounds). Cases of cancer and infertility in Iraq have risen dramatically, and some doctors fear that weapons used in the war could create genetic abnormalities which will dog families for generations to come.

🅠 Are burgers really bad for you?

🅐 The average quarter-pounder is a good source of protein, iron, zinc, Vitamin B12 and niacin; and it's not too bad at delivering calcium, along with Vitamins B6, B2 and C. What makes it less good for you is that it is also high in fats, especially saturated fats. And too much of those in your diet will lead to obesity and heart disease.

Take a McDonald's Quarter Pounder, which the company says is "100 per cent pure beef, prime cuts of lean forequarter and flank with no additives, fillers, binders or flavour enhancers". That burger contains 509 calories; a fifth of a man's Recommended Daily Allowance (RDA) of 2,550 calories, and a quarter of a woman's (1,940 calories). It also has 26.3g of protein – 59 per cent of the RDA for men (71 per cent for women) – excess protein is stored in the body as fat. The burger's carbohydrate levels are quite low, at just 25.2g; 8 per cent of the RDA. But the amount of fat is high; 24.9g, half of which is saturated, making up 25 per cent of his RDA and 33 per cent of hers. That's a fat lot of fat in one quickly digested snack. The best advice would be to eat them by all means, but don't eat too many of them. A burger every once in a while is fine but don't let them become your staple diet.

It's pretty hard to avoid the things, mind you. McDonald's operates in 91 countries – which is almost half the countries in the world. You might think that India, where the Hindu faith prohibits the eating of beef, would be McDonald's-free, but Delhi now boasts the world's first McDonald's where there is no beef is sight but you can buy a Maharaja Mac (yes, really) made with lamb.

Still, there are 101 countries where Ronald McDonald hasn't got to yet, including Nepal, the Seychelles, Afghanistan, Libya, North Korea, Iraq and Iran.

🔵 what is the least nutritious fast food?

🔴 All food is nutritious to some degree – it's how you include it in your overall diet that matters. Chips, for example, are a fairly good source of Vitamin C – a 100g portion gives you 4mg, or about 10 per cent of your Recommended Daily Allowance (RDA) – but the downside is that they're very high in fat. To get your daily 40mg dose of Vitamin C from them, you would have to eat your way through 2,750 calories' worth of chips – which would also contain a whopping 140g of fat.

If you really want a coronary, go for a half-pound cheeseburger with large fries and a milkshake, says Dr Tim Lobstein, co-director of the Food Commission and author of *Fast Food Facts*. Onion bhajis, Chinese spare ribs, fried chicken and pork pies are pretty terrible as well. If you must indulge, he says, then opt for a pizza with plenty of base (good for protein and calcium) and not so much cheese, or a shish kebab (again, lots of protein and calcium, plus iron, zinc and vitamins).

🔵 How long after someone sneezes can you catch their virus?

🔴 According to Professor Ron Eccles, Director of the Common Cold Centre at Cardiff University, when someone sneezes, droplets containing viruses spray out just for a short distance and stay around for just a matter of seconds. If they make contact with your eyes or nose during this time, then you are immediately at risk of infection.

There is another possible means of transmission, though, which is not so instant: some of the particles emitted when someone sneezes do linger in the air, as an aerosol, for several hours. It's thought unlikely that you'll catch a cold by coming into contact with this aerosol but it may be an efficient way of transmitting the flu virus.

🎯 Is there any point letting red wine "breathe"?

🍷 Not much – apart from maybe fooling your guests into thinking that you know something about wine. Removing the cork for half-an-hour prior to serving is certainly pretty pointless, as the volume of wine exposed to the air is negligible compared to the volume of the wine in the bottle.

Decanting wine does a better job of mixing the wine with surrounding air and, according to *Decanter* magazine, this allows the aromas and flavours to develop. Well, maybe – but in blind tests even experts can't consistently discern any real difference between "breathed" and "non-breathed" wines.

🎯 Is red wine good for you?

🍷 The idea that red wine is good for combating heart disease has been swilling around in the medical world for years. The claims tend to focus on the fact that red wine is rich in catechin, which belongs to a group of chemicals called flavonoids. These are thought to protect against free radicals, highly reactive fragments of molecules that can contribute to coronary heart disease. It's a nice idea, but it all falls apart on closer inspection.

A study by scientists at the University of California compared the concentrations of catechin in the blood of people after they had consumed alcoholic and alcohol-free wine. The concentrations rose sharply in both cases, but dropped much faster after being taken in wine. This may be because the alcohol caused the catechin to be excreted or metabolised more quickly than in the non-alcoholic sample.

Examining all the evidence for the benefits of red wine, the American Heart Association has decided that it just doesn't stack up. In January 2001 the AHA issued a blunt statement that the idea of red wine being good for the heart is a "popular but unproven supposition".

why do we like junk food?

Despite the fact that we have access to virtually any food we could possibly want, the Western diet still contains far more sweet and fat food than is good for us. The idea that we are still locked into the diet we had when we were Ice-Age cavemen just doesn't stand up: humans have never needed so much "junk" in their diet. One current theory is that junk food reminds us of the great taste of breast milk, which is both sweet and contains around 40 per cent fat – strikingly similar to the levels in the Western diet.

is it true that fatty food gives you spots?

Good news: you can chomp away on as many chips, fry-ups and chocolate bars as you like and you won't get spots. They're actually caused by high levels of hormones, which trigger over-production of grease by the skin. What you eat won't make the slightest difference.

What does make a difference is puberty, when levels of these hormones reach new heights, leading to blocked-up pores and the dreaded acne. Of course, lots of spotty teenagers also eat lots of chocolate and fatty foods – which may explain how this myth got started.

when were the first artificial limbs invented?

Wooden legs have been in use since Roman times, but the first realistic-looking artificial limbs – "prostheses" – were developed by the sixteenth-century French surgeon Ambroise Paré. One of Paré's prosthetic hand designs had fingers that could be moved individually via a set of gears and levers.

The two World Wars gave added impetus to the design of many artificial limbs, as many more soldiers survived amputations, thanks to better military medicine. New, lightweight materials and better mechanical joints were introduced, initially for the lower limb, with further advances in upper arm prostheses after World War II. Artificial hips were first developed in the early years of the twentieth century, although hip replacement operations didn't become routine until the 1970s.

However sophisticated the prosthesis, it is of limited use unless it fits well. The latest refinement is the Hanger Comfort Flex socket, made of a smart plastic that can "remember" the shape of a person's residual limb to give an exact fit. The socket contains contoured, anatomically designed channels and grooves to accommodate the muscle, bone, tendon, blood vessels and nerve areas of the residual limb. Inside, the socket is flexible, giving better side-to-side control and front-to-back stability. It's also more comfortable for the wearer, because it prevents the prosthesis from rotating in the socket and stops pressure from concentrating on any one point of the residual limb. People who've been fitted with this socket find they can control the prosthesis more effectively. This in turn lets them get back to work and become more involved in other physical activities such as sports.

can I protect myself from harmful radiation in the home or office?

Sure – although you may well suffer more ill-health from just fretting about the radiation than by anything it's actually doing to you. Computers, mobile phones, TVs and microwave ovens all produce electromagnetic radiation (EMR), but the evidence that any of it does harm at the levels found in the home and office is equivocal, to say the least.

That's not stopped companies coming up with remedies, of course. These include a range of special clothing with silver-plated nylon fibres sewn into the fabric and special pockets for mobile phones. The fibres, developed in America, allegedly cut out up to 99 per cent of high frequency radiation emitted by electronic equipment.

why do guinness bubbles sink?

The rapidly falling bubbles in a pint of Guinness have baffled many a drinker in the past. After all, aren't bubbles less dense than the surrounding liquid – and shouldn't they therefore rise? Scientists at the University of New South Wales, Sydney, Australia, have used computational fluid-dynamics software to find the answer.

It turns out that most Guinness bubbles do in fact go upwards in the centre of the glass, but are hidden by the darkness of the brew. Trapped in each bubble is a tiny amount of fluid. At the surface, the gas escapes but the fluid is pushed sideways, hitting the edge of the glass and sending the current back down the inside walls. These are the bubbles seen by the Guinness tippler.

Ireland's best-known beverage is more susceptible to this than other drinks as the smaller the bubble, the easier it is to be pulled to the bottom. And according to Professor Clive Fletcher, who headed the research at the university, Guinness has a high concentration of small bubbles and is more viscous than other beers.

why do we associate the colour blue with being sad?

There are all sorts of explanations: psychological, mythological and scientific. Perhaps the most interesting answer to this question comes from behavioural tests using coloured wooden blocks carried out on chimpanzees in West Africa.

The study found that chimps preferred blue or grey coloured blocks on days when the weather was bad, when they were hungry or when they had been separated from the group. On the day that one of the chimps died of illness, all the other chimps wanted to pick up blue wooden blocks.

The mythological explanation is that blue is the colour of the sea, the object of much fear and dread among ancient man (the

Great Beast rose from the sea in the *Book of Revelations*, for example).

Another intriguing link between depression and the colour blue comes from a report in a nineteenth-century journal of psychology, which said that a study had discovered that "dyers working with indigo became melancholic."

How do painkillers "know" where the pain is?

Painkillers home in on an enzyme that appears only at the site of an injury. The enzyme, called cyclo-oxygenase, (COX), causes the local production of chemicals called prostaglandins, which amplify pain signals. Simple analgesics, such as aspirin, paracetamol or ibuprofen, are designed to chemically lock on to COX, blocking its function and so stopping the prostaglandins being made.

When you have a headache, the injury is to the membranes covering the brain which have become stretched or distorted. This can happen when blood vessels in the skull dilate – often as a result of a night on the tiles.

Paracetamol is by far the most popular painkiller in the UK with around 130 million packs sold each year. Take too much though and you'll have something worse than a headache: potentially lethal liver damage. Each year, around 100 people die in the UK from suicidal overdoses of paracetamol.

What is phantom pain?

Pain can be experienced as coming from a body part that no longer exists. Around two-thirds of people who have had limbs amputated report intense sensations apparently originating from where the limb used to be. This so-called phantom pain has nothing to do with any discomfort from the amputation procedure. It can be very distressing, however, often persisting for many years after a damaged or diseased body part has been removed. The explanation for it may be that the brain becomes confused by the lack of input from the absent part of the body.

Much more common but no less bizarre is the phenomenon of referred pain, where pain is perceived as coming from a part of the body other than the one in trouble. For example, the pain of a heart attack is often felt in the left shoulder, arm or hand. And recently, it's emerged that women experience the pain of a heart attack differently from men – often they misinterpret it as a sports injury, possibly involving the back.

Why referred pain occurs is unclear. It may be because nerves from both regions feed into a common pool of neurons, or that the origin of the signal becomes confused by the brain.

will there ever be a panacea?

A cure for all ills sounds like the stuff of legend, but there's already a compound that comes pretty close – aspirin. In its natural form of salicylic acid – a compound found in willow bark – it has been used as a remedy for pain and fever since the days of the great Greek physician Hippocrates (470–377BC).

By the nineteenth century, salicylic acid was a popular remedy for rheumatic fever, gout and arthritis. But it also caused stomach irritation and some people developed ulcers. Felix Hoffman, a German chemist at the drug company Bayer, modified salicylic acid to produce aspirin, which went on sale as the first ever pharmaceutical drug in 1899. However, even aspirin can irritate the stomach if used in high doses because, besides blocking the pain-producing enzyme COX, it also blocks one that produces stomach mucus.

A century on, and the first of the "superaspirin" drugs – known as COX-2 inhibitors – are now entering the market. These block only the pain-producing enzyme. Over the years, aspirin has proved useful in more than just pain relief, however. Evidence has been uncovered for its value in preventing heart attacks and strokes. It may even help protect against Alzheimer's disease and some cancers.

Health, medicine and nutrition

☺ what's the point of pain?

☻ Pain may be unpleasant but it does have a purpose. Medical science has recorded around one hundred instances of a genetic defect called congenital analgesia, which leaves people unable to feel pain. They have to navigate their way through life trying not to do things that would cause an injury – because they have no way of telling if they are suffering from one.

The best-documented case of congenital analgesia was of the daughter of a Canadian doctor who soon developed severe damage to her knees, hips and spine, because she never felt any knocks or bumps. Her father recalled how one day she knelt on a boiling hot radiator during the freezing Canadian winter without recoiling – and bore the scars on her knees for the rest of her short life. A life of repetitive minor injury soon took its toll. Damaged tissue in the girl's wrists, knees and ankles became a breeding ground for bacteria, which ate through to the bone. She died of a virtually untreatable bone infection, osteomyelitis, aged just 22.

Such extreme cases have an important lesson for the rest of us: don't take pain-killers for symptoms that last for more than a day or so. Pain is usually the result of something having gone wrong with your body – so taking pain-killers regularly is like switching off a burglar alarm before checking whether or not your home has actually been burgled.

☺ How can I cook a chicken or turkey to perfection?

☻ For many people, Christmas dinner is the best part of the big day – and making a mess of it causes all sorts of trouble. The most common mistake is not cooking the turkey for long enough, so that it ends up being served tough and chewy.

Cooking a turkey or chicken to perfection depends on rules that come from a combination of two sciences; biochemistry and physics. If the bird isn't roasted for long enough, the strands of collagen making up its muscles don't turn into tender gelatin, leaving it horribly chewy. But if the roasting goes on for too long, then coagulation sets in, causing muscle proteins to link up with each other, again producing a tough old bird.

To avoid both, the bird has to be cooked long enough and hot enough to ensure that all of it reaches a temperature of around 70°C, at which collagen turns to gelatin. Of course, the heavier the turkey, the longer it takes for the heat to work its way through to the centre. Working out how much longer it will need is a physics problem and heat diffusion theory shows that the cooking time varies according to the two-thirds power of the turkey's mass. This sounds very complex but, fortunately, the simple chefs' rule of an hour per kilogram at 180°C amounts to just the same thing.

How does schizophrenia cause split personality?

It doesn't. Indeed, it's amazing how many people still think schizophrenia is anything to do with split personalities. The name is a problem: "schizo" does indeed mean "split", but with schizophrenia the split is between the intellect and the emotions, not personalities. It's true that so-called multiple personality disorders do exist, with people having a "split personality" – but these are incredibly rare.

People with schizophrenia have problems telling what is real and what isn't and to that extent, schizophrenics are suffering from the classic form of "madness", a psychosis where they lose touch with reality. Terrifyingly, when they hear voices in their heads, or have visual hallucinations, it's as real as if someone is actually talking to or being with them. Schizophrenics can also become entirely convinced that someone intends to do them harm, or wants them to harm others.

⚥ Do dangly chains cure car sickness?

⚥ Remarkably, you still see cars with these things hanging off the back, supposedly curing car sickness by getting rid of "static electricity". The whole idea is nonsense, of course; car sickness is caused by the conflict between what your eyes are seeing, and what your balance system tells you is actually happening. On winding roads, for example, your eyes may be looking straight ahead, but your inner ear will be sensing the change in direction as you go round the corners. The disparity triggers the release of stress hormones and makes your stomach churn – and before long you start to feel anxious and queasy. The best advice to avoid car sickness is to keep your eyes fixed on the road ahead but lean into the curves.

⚥ Why can't doctors just glue broken bones back together?

⚥ Doctors have long dreamed of using glue instead of the pins and bolts traditionally used to repair broken bones. The trouble is that most adhesives only work on dry surfaces. There is a glue that performs astonishingly well in the wet, however – the mucus that mussels exude, allowing them to stick to rocks in water. One species, *Mytilus galloprovincialis*, produces a protein twice as resilient as man-made adhesives containing epoxy resins.

Dr Simon McQueen-Mason of York University says the glue protein works in wet conditions because its flexible structure allows it to get into microscopic gaps in the surface it is bonding to, and at the same time exclude oxygen and water molecules. McQueen-Mason's team believes that it can mass-produce the protein by transferring the gene that encodes for its production from mussels into tobacco plants to be harvested. The glue could then be put to commercial use. As the protein is naturally occurring, it would almost certainly not damage cells as many synthetic products can.

why won't my doctor give me antibiotics for my cold?

Because antibiotics are useless against colds. Antibiotics are compounds that kill bacteria: microscopic bugs that cause diseases such as TB, pneumonia and gonorrhoea. Colds and influenza, on the other hand, are caused by viruses, against which antibiotics have absolutely no effect.

Some patients think they know better, however, and demand antibiotics every time they have a bit of a sore throat. It's true that some sore throats are the result of bacterial infections, but doctors who hand out antibiotics to such patients usually just want an easy time. Such cavalier use of antibiotics has helped create mutant bacteria that are developing resistance to all known antibiotics – which is not a happy prospect at all.

How many bacteria are there on my skin?

Oh, just a few billion or so – some of which can kill you if ingested in large quantities. They're known in the trade as micrococci and around 30 per cent of us have a particularly nasty variety, *Staphylococcus*, breeding on our hands. Most of the time our skin keeps these bugs at bay with the various bacteria-zapping chemicals it exudes, such as lysozyme. But cut yourself, and you could find that you are instantly invaded by *Staphylococcus aureus*, the micrococcus that causes boils and abscesses.

Then there's *Streptococcus pyogenes*, a very nasty and resistant variety which caused about a dozen fatalities in 1994, during the "Killer Bacteria Ate My Face" episode in Gloucestershire. In 1941 PC Albert Alexander from Oxford fell victim to both *Staphylococcus aureus* and *Streptococcus pyogenes* after pricking himself with a rose-thorn – and became the first person to be treated with antibiotics. Tragically, the doctors ran out of the newly-developed penicillin before they could cure him.

health, medicine and nutrition

🅠 why is spinach so amazingly good for you?

🅐 Well, it is quite good for you – but the fact is that spinach really got its reputation as a wonder-food as the result of a misprint. It all began in 1870, when a German nutritionist was analysing the iron content of foods. While recording his result for spinach, he misplaced the decimal point. At a stroke, he had boosted the iron content of this boring leaf vegetable by a factor of ten – and the legend of Spinach the Wonder-food was born.

By 1929, the American cartoonist Elzie Segar had created the spinach-wolfing character Popeye, and kids everywhere were being encouraged to eat heaps of the stuff. In fact, spinach has perfectly ordinary levels of iron. That said, it is an excellent source of folic acid – which is great for pregnant mothers. That fact doesn't quite have the same superhero ring to it, though, does it?

🅠 what was "dancing mania"?

🅐 Of all the mystery madnesses to have gripped apparently sane people, the most famous are the outbreaks of "dancing mania" that flared up many times across Europe from around 1350 to 1700.

Entire towns would suddenly become filled with people seized with an insatiable desire to literally dance till they dropped, for days, even weeks, collapsing on the ground with exhaustion and convulsions before starting all over again.

Medieval Italy had its own peculiar form of dancing mania, known as tarantism – supposedly triggered by the bite of the spider, *Lycosa tarantula*. Those thinking that they had been bitten – or somehow "infected" by a victim – would dance for days on end before deciding they were cured.

Some researchers have argued that such dancing manias were a mass response to the huge psychological stress under which peasants lived, caused by crop failures, plague, wars and social misery on a scale unimaginable today. Yet others have pointed to a far simpler explanation: during the Medieval period, there was a popular belief that dancing near religious shrines – especially those of St Vitus, a Sicilian boy martyred in the 4th century – could secure good health for a year. Suddenly "dancing mania" becomes no more baffling than trips to Mecca by Muslims.

However, some social historians have suggested that dancing mania was really a form of mass protest by an otherwise powerless section of the community. As an example, they cite the case of one of the most famous outbreaks of the mania, in Liège, France, in 1374. This coincided with general disenchantment with the hypocrisy of the local clergy, who preached chastity while keeping concubines. The locals, who deemed their baptisms to be invalid, duly became "possessed" by demons, and broke out in wild dancing – forcing the clergy to tear themselves away from their mistresses and pay more attention to their flock.

why don't we drink pig's milk?

Pigs are well known for having just about every part of their bodies used for something: their bristles in shaving-brushes, their skin in wallets, their meat cured for our breakfast. And as pigs' organs (except their brains) are similar in size to those of humans, scientists are even genetically engineering pigs, in order that they may one day be used to provide transplant organs for humans.

So why don't we also use their milk? It's not because of the taste; pigs belong to the same order of mammals as goats, sheep and cattle, and their milk tastes similar. The real reason we don't get our daily pint of pig's milk is, according to the Milk Development Council, far more simple – it's the devil's own job to milk a pig. Unlike their farmyard cousins, pigs don't have udders; instead, they have teats – and so far, it's not proved worthwhile to develop the equipment needed to extract milk from them.

🤖 Why do we feel sick when someone else vomits?

🅰 There are few things worse than having that heaving sensation in your guts while someone else is in the process of throwing up beside you. What's happening is that your stomach is reacting in sympathy. It is a primeval defence merchanism designed to protect you against poisoning. Just a few thousand years ago, if your friend had eaten something that didn't agree with them, it would have been likely that you had eaten some too.

The vagus nerve is the thing that's to blame, as it acts as a channel through which the body's sympathetic nervous system sends a physiological stimulus from the brain down to your stomach. Running through the chest and around the stomach wall, the vagus nerve activates the acid-secreting cells in the stomach. Usually, it's triggered as food hits your belly, but it can also be set in motion as part of an emotional response. So, as your mate is retching, your brain is putting your body into "fear and flight" mode. Your heart beats faster, you start sweating, saliva collects in your mouth and acid pumps into your stomach, making you want to vomit. And there's very little you can do about it.

🤖 How does salt help to clean wounds?

🅰 Common salt (sodium chloride) was once administered to wounds for the same reason it was prized as a food preservative for thousands of years: it kills bacteria – in pretty much the same way as it kills slugs. Salt creates a concentration of dissolved ions outside bacteria cells that draws water out across their membranes by osmosis. The bacteria then either die or their reproduction rate greatly declines.

In the days before antiseptics, surgical patients were almost as likely to die from infections as they were from their original illness. Patients were willing to suffer the terrible pain of having salt applied to their injuries – caused as it dries out all cells, not just bacteria – to ward off the deadly threat of gangrene.

Royal Navy surgeons applied salt to the wounds of flogged sailors, though it hurt so much that the sailors considered it just as much a part of the punishment as the flogging itself. This is where the phrase "rubbing salt into the wound" originally comes from.

Since the introduction of surgical antiseptics in 1860, treatments have been developed – such as the "surgical spirit" ethanol – that have the same effect without the irritation.

How safe are you in your own home?

Less safe than you'd think. Around 2.5 million of us injure ourselves at home every year, according to the Royal Society for the Prevention of Accidents. Trips, slips and falls are the most common accidents. And the place where they most often happen? The stairs.

Hurting yourself in the garden is also very common. Bedrooms are almost as dangerous – around 300,000 of us annually report injuries inflicted by beds. More than 13,000 people (mostly children) find that jumping off wardrobes is really quite a bad idea, while putting on socks when standing on a highly polished floor, or taking them off while drunk, is also risky – every year, about 7,000 people end up in hospital that way.

The bathroom can also be dangerous – and not just for those who like to watch telly in the bath. Every year, some people are brave enough to tell the hospital staff they were injured by their toothpaste. About 500 people are attacked by their toothbrush, and 2,500 by their towels. In the kitchen, a couple of people a year manage to injure themselves with tea-cosies. But only 4,000 injuries a year are caused by high chairs, whereas injury by "sofa, couch or ottoman" causes a massive 35,000 people to visit the hospital.

How does popcorn pop?

A kernel of popcorn (the small brown seed) contains a drop of water, which is stored inside a circle of soft starch. So, when the kernel is heated, the water turns to steam, putting huge pressure on the hard surface of the kernel. Eventually it gives way, causing the popcorn to explode. As it does so, the soft starch becomes inflated, turning the kernel inside out and creating fluffy popcorn.

What causes epilepsy?

The short answer is that nobody knows. About 1 in 200 people suffer from epilepsy, in which the brain is suddenly gripped by violent electrical discharges. In some cases, doctors can find abnormalities in the brains of epileptics, caused by problems from diseases such as meningitis or brain cancer, or simple drug abuse. But in many more there seems to be nothing wrong at all. Drugs that block the electrical activity that causes seizures and even removal of the damaged part of the brain by surgery have both proved successful treatments. And in some cases, particularly among children, the disorder seems to disappear as mysteriously as it arrived.

What was the Plague of Athens?

Around 430BC, an appalling disease struck Athens, killing 300,000 people. According to the historian Thucydides – who survived an attack of the illness – the first symptoms were a burning sensation in the head and stinging eyes, followed by a hacking cough, vomiting and blistered skin. Most victims died within a week.

Nothing quite like it has been seen since, although recently a team of American researchers claimed that it may have been an outbreak of the dreaded *Ebola* virus, which killed over 200 people in Zaire in 1995.

Is cancer contagious?

For many years, medical scientists refused to believed that cancer could be infectious. But now millions of people are known to die each year after becoming infected with cancer-causing viruses.

Cancer of the liver, white blood cells and the lymph system have all been linked to viruses, with the Human Papilloma Virus (HPV) alone killing over 1,000 women in the UK each year from cervical cancer. HPV is spread among women via their male sexual partners, who can carry the virus without any obvious symptoms. Invading the cells lining the cervix, the virus causes the cells to malfunction, producing cervical cancer 20 years or more after infection.

Doctors suspect that following the sexual revolution of the 1960s, huge numbers of women became infected with HPV – leading to cervical cancer becoming the most common sexually transmitted disease among British women, killing well over ten times more each year than AIDS.

Can armadillos really help to cure leprosy?

While attempting to unravel the secrets of leprosy, scientists have been forced to recruit an unusual helper: the armadillo. The leprosy bacterium does not survive in a Petri dish or in most animals, and for decades, living human flesh was the only source for scientists wanting to study the devious little microbe.

However, after realising that leprosy thrives in the coolest sections of a human body, researchers managed to infect the cool footpads of mice and the ears of hamsters with leprosy in the 1960s. Researchers in the United States then wondered whether armadillos, which have a body temperature five degrees lower than most mammals, might be a host for the disease.

Unfortunately for armadillos, early experiments proved the researchers right. When infected, armadillos are completely overpowered by the disease: one animal yields one million times as many leprosy bacilli as a mouse footpad. The huge quantities of bacteria have allowed scientists to test new drugs. They have also been extracted and used to prepare a substance called lepromin. This can determine whether an individual has been exposed to leprosy and to predict the likely course of the disease so doctors can plan its treatment.

In recent years wild armadillos infected with leprosy have been found in the US, and some doctors are concerned that the creatures could cause a major outbreak of the disease among humans in the future.

what basic advice can make us healthier?

"Go to work on an egg"..."drink a pint of milk every day"..."too much cholesterol increases your risk of heart disease"...what should we take and what should we leave when it comes to health advice? The things we are told to do seem to change almost as frequently as the weather. Well, there are some pieces of health advice that do remain constant. Doctors are unanimous about certain things and although we all think we know them, many people, especially men, still fail to follow them.

In Britain, we could drastically cut our intake of sugar and fat – particularly animal derived, saturated fat. We should also consume more complex carbohydrates from fresh fruit and vegetables. The biggest killer in the UK, after smoking, is a diet rich in meat and animal products such as milk and cheese. A good diet should include five to seven portions of fresh fruit and vegetables a day. Protein and energy-giving carbohydrates should come from whole grains and pulses such as lentils and beans.

The only fat should come from that found naturally in whole, unprocessed foods. If fat is needed, it should be derived from such wholesome sources as extra virgin olive oil. If you still think you might need supplements, stick to the recommended daily doses for each vitamin and mineral, which are given on the bottles.

🅠 Is decaffeinated coffee harmful?

🅐 A true decaffeinated coffee must contain less than 0.1 per cent caffeine (against 1 to 1.5 per cent in normal coffee). This means that in a single cup of decaffeinated coffee there are only 10mg of caffeine compared with 80mg in a shot of espresso and 150mg in a standard cup of filter coffee brewed at home.

Caffeine, of course, acts as a stimulant, and raises your blood pressure. This is why decaffeinated coffee is recommended to cardiac patients and people with hypertension in particular. However, it has been suggested that decaffeinated coffee may contain harmful residues produced by the decaffeination process.

This might have been true some time ago, when that process involved chemical solvents, but today only water or carbon monoxide is used. The still-green coffee beans are put into a watertight container and sprayed with jets of liquid which makes the caffeine soluble. The caffeine then flows down through a waste pipe and the beans are roasted and dried.

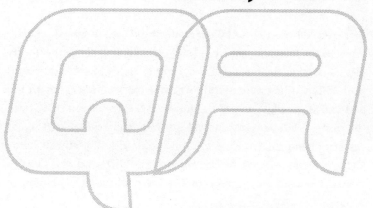

maths,
money and
amazing
numbers

How many people die on the planet each day?

According to statistics from the London-based charity Population Concern, the world's average death rate currently stands at nine deaths per 1,000 people each year. As the world population is just over six billion, that works out at a death toll of 148,000 people each day – almost two per second. However, the daily death rate can increase dramatically because of major catastrophes – such as the 1 million people killed by storms in the Ganges Delta islands of Bangladesh in 1970, and the 800,000 deaths from an earthquake in the town of Shaanxi, China, in 1556.

Disease epidemics can also cause huge increases in death-rates that last for decades: between 1347 and 1351, the Black Death killed around 25 million in Europe alone, reducing the population of the world at the time by over 25 per cent. The Aids epidemic, which has so far killed over 16 million people, has also been a major cause of increasing death rates over the last 20 years, especially in sub-Saharan Africa.

Worldwide, the average death rate has fallen by 10 per cent since the early 1990s – though this crude statistic hides the contrasts between the rich and poor. For example, Japan's annual death rate per 1,000 is 30 per cent lower than the world's average; but in Central Africa, death rates often exceed twice the average, not least because of Aids.

Where should you buy property in monopoly?

First invented in America in the mid-1930s, the property game Monopoly still sells around 300,000 sets each year. The aim is to acquire land, build properties and extract rent from other players until they all go bankrupt. For most people, it's just a game – but inevitably some take it a lot more seriously, and have tried to work out the best places to buy property.

The trick would seem to be to pick those sites that generate the most revenue because they have high rents, and those that people land on most frequently. But as players end up on sites dictated by the throw of dice, the latter strategy would seem hopeless – you would think that every square should be visited at random as often as any other. Well, this is not quite the case, because two dice are used. That means that on average people move by seven squares on each throw (as there are more ways of coming up with the number seven from two dice than any other number). And that allows the best sites to be identified using a branch of maths called Markov Chain theory. Essentially a way of predicting what is likely to happen given what has just happened, Markov Chain theory can be used to work out which squares players are most likely to land on after throwing the two dice from the same starting point – the Go square – and thus the best playing strategies.

In 1997, the American mathematician Tom Friddell used Markov Chain theory to confirm Monopoly folklore that Trafalgar Square is the single most landed-on square, making it very profitable to players who acquire it along with the two other red properties, Fleet Street and Strand. The orange sites of Vine Street, Marlborough Street and Bow Street also emerged as frequently-visited sites, with Marylebone station the most visited – and thus most profitable – station, and Water Works the most profitable utility. At the other end of the spectrum is lowly Whitechapel Road, the least-visited, and thus least desirable, site on the entire board.

Friddell's calculations also revealed that players should focus on developing their properties to three houses per site before going on to build more houses or hotels, as this allows investments to be covered by rents relatively quickly, and thus protects against bankruptcy.

⊙ Are there any codes that are impossible to break?

⊙ In these days of "teraflop" computers capable of a thousand billion operations a second, it seems impossible for any secret message to stay secret for long. Yet, a code invented decades before the first computer was built can resist attack by even the most powerful computers imaginable. In fact, it's been mathematically proven to be unbreakable (and so far, it's the only one with that accolade). It is called the one-time system.

Invented in 1918 by the US Army code expert Major Joseph Mauborgne, it could hardly be simpler: you just write your message down, convert each letter to a number (say, 1 for A, up to 26 for Z), and then add a randomly-chosen number between 0 and 9 to each one. The resulting jumbling cannot be unjumbled. However, once a certain sequence of random numbers has been used, it must never be used again – which is why the system is called "one-time".

So why isn't everyone using the one-time system? Basically, the reason is because the random numbers need to be truly random, and that's very difficult to achieve – certainly the "random" numbers generated by computers aren't good enough. Worse, when suitably random numbers have been created, they have to be sent to the receiver before any messages can be decoded – raising the risk of the list of numbers being intercepted. Worst of all is the fact that each precious list must only be used once and then destroyed – a key rule the Soviet Union broke during the Second World War, with disastrous consequences for its network of spies. American code-breakers analysing intercepted Soviet messages realised that a list of random numbers had been used twice and were able to "break" some of the messages. This led to the unmasking of some of the most famous spies of the twentieth century, such as the atom spy Laus Fuchs and the KGB's "Magnificent Five": Kim Philby, Donald Maclean, Guy Burgess, Anthony Blunt and John Cairncross.

Most code systems used today aren't provably unbreakable – but they are thought to be so hard to break that the information they conceal should be useless by the time the code is cracked. Yet, despite the huge research effort that goes into finding new code systems, even messages using very simple codes can defeat the most powerful code-breaking computer – provided they are short enough.

Back in 1949, the American mathematician Claude Shannon applied his newly-invented concept of Information Theory to the question of keeping messages secret. He showed that below a certain length of text, even very simple randomly-jumbled codes – where, for example, G always stands for "E" and H is always "P" – can be unbreakable if they're used to encode just a few words. The reason is that there just isn't enough information for the code-breaker to be certain that the most common code-letter really does represent "E" and so on. As a result, some of the cryptic messages on gravestones containing just a few coded letters will forever remain unreadable – except to those with the secret key.

what's the best way of getting out of a maze?

For many famous old mazes – like the ones at Hampton Court, or Hever Castle in Kent – it's possible to find your way in to the centre and back out again just by keeping one hand in constant touch with one wall of the maze as you tramp round within it. But beware; this is not a very fast method, and may well take you in and out via a very long route.

With more modern mazes, such as those at Blenheim in Oxfordshire, or Leeds Castle in Kent, the one-hand-on-the-wall trick doesn't work. Their designers were aware of the method and made traps for people who might use it.

A more reliable way of finding your way in and out is known as Tremaux's Method, which works as follows: whenever you come to a new junction, take any route off it you like and back-track only if it leads to a junction you've been to before or a dead-end. If you come to an old junction by a path you've taken once before, then this time take a new path off it if possible; otherwise, take a path used not more than once before. But whatever you do, never take the same path twice.

Surprisingly, this rigmarole has some use beyond helping people get out of mazes before closing time. Methods for getting out of mazes belong to a field of mathematics called Graph Theory, which can help sort out some of the tricky questions of organising big projects. For example, in the 1950s, the US Navy used Graph Theory to guide its multi-billion dollar Polaris nuclear submarine program. Today, ideas such as Critical Path Analysis are used by manufacturing companies to get products to market in the shortest possible time.

A major breakthrough in Graph Theory came in 1989, when mathematicians discovered the so-called Depth First Algorithm – a recipe for finding the best solution to a host of Graph Theory problems. Despite its fancy name, after analysis it turned out to be identical to Tremaux's Method of escaping from mazes.

what is the best way to choose lottery numbers?

Many people think it doesn't matter how you choose your six numbers, as any of the 49 balls has just as much chance as any other of popping out of the lottery machine. This is true, but if you want to maximise your winnings when you do pick the jackpot numbers, it pays to choose very carefully. It could make the difference between, say, £16 million to yourself – or sharing it with scores of others. Just ask the winners of one of the early Lottery jackpots in 1995 – there were 133 of them, all of whom chose 7, 17, 23, 32, 38 and 42, and thus won just £120,000 each.

In 1998, a team of scientists at Southampton University revealed that the most commonly chosen set of numbers was 7, 17, 23, 32, 40 and 42, while the least common is 26, 34, 44, 46, 47 and 49. So should you switch to this last set, if you want to maximise your winnings if the number does come up? Well, no, not now – because chances are that a lot of people reading this book will do the same, thus ruining your chances of winning outright!

The best system for picking your numbers is no system at all – you should make your selection as random as possible. Using your birthday to choose numbers is not a good idea: after all, thousands of other people were born on the same day, and they might be using the same system. Trying to think up random numbers is not easy, however. Most people are hopeless at it, and produce selections with far too little "clustering". Clustering is very common in random numbers; John Haigh of Sussex University has proved mathematically that roughly half of all Lottery draws contain a pair of consecutive numbers such as 15 and 16. Yet most people avoid pairs and tend to choose mostly low numbers.

In the end, the best way to generate your numbers is not to get yourself involved at all. Just let the National Lottery's own Lucky Dip random number generator pick six for you.

How can you tell what money used to be worth?

We've all heard old folks complain how their job only paid £25 a week – hoping that we don't realise that everything cost less back then too. The reason that £1 buys less today than it did 10 years ago is inflation, which eats away at our buying-power. It's a spiral which involves price rises triggering higher wage demands, which in turn pushes up the costs of products, causing prices to rise still higher. Inflation has been around for thousands of years: even the Roman Empire had it. The rate, however, can vary dramatically. In the UK during the mid-1970s, the rate of inflation reached 25 per cent a year; currently it runs at around 3 per cent or so.

The effect of inflation on past buying-power can be roughly estimated using the following benchmarks: £1 was worth twice as much in 1983, five times more in 1975, 10 times more in 1968, 20 times more in 1949, 100 times more in 1727, and 500 times more in 1500.

Even when inflation rates are low – as they currently are – your buying-power is still being nibbled away. Working out by how much – and thus what size of pay-rise you should get – is very simple, however. You just take the amount of time that has passed since your last pay rise and multiply it by the average percentage inflation rate over that period. For example, if you haven't had a pay-rise for the last five years, you can roughly estimate how much to ask for by multiplying five by around 3 per cent, giving 15 per cent. So put in for 20 per cent – the chances are that your boss won't think of checking your calculations.

🔵 Is there any way to predict a coincidence?

🔵 Coincidences are the result of chance, making them subject to the laws of probability – and these often serve to show that coincidences are much more likely than you think. For example, there's a better than 50 per cent chance that in a gathering of just 23 people at least two will share the same birthday, while there are almost as good odds of at least two people sharing the same star-sign in a group of just four.

Using probability theory, one of the editors of this book had a go at predicting how many coincidences of various kinds would be found among the players and officials of the Premiership football matches that took place one Saturday in 1997. Theory predicted that there would be five matches that day featuring players who shared the same birthday; in fact, there were six. The same theory also predicted that there would be one match with two sets of shared birthdays; in fact, there were two. It also predicted there'd be one match where a player or official would be celebrating a birthday that very weekend – and sure enough, there was one.

So, armed with a bit of maths, it is possible to show that many coincidences aren't as spooky as they seem – and that they may even be predictable.

what is the most expensive hotel room in the world?

At a whopping $25,000 a night for the Galactica Suite, the Crystal Palace Hotel in the Bahamas tops the bill. For this ludicrous sum, you get a set of rooms decked out with enough gear to satisfy the most demanding gadget freak.

Pushing buttons does a lot more than just dimming lights or changing TV channels: your bed or sofa rotates, a giant aquarium lights up, sculptures appear to come to life, virtual thunderstorms erupt, stars shoot across the ceiling, and finally, a giant video screen bursts into life.

Thrown in at no extra charge is Ursula the robot – a Grace Jones-style android with a breathless voice like Marilyn Monroe. Programmed to respond to your every whim with unfailing electronic efficiency, she has an army of butlers, chambermaids and maîtres d'hôtel to assist her. As she's at your side every minute of the day, Ursula can store and update your personal tastes and preferences in her memory bank, and therefore anticipate your every need. Even in the immense bathroom – which is extravagantly kitted out with steam baths, saunas and the very latest in Jacuzzi technology – Ursula stands by with a soft towel at the ready, her "eyes" turned tactfully towards the ceiling.

which parasite bug has wreaked the most havoc in history?

A tiny rod-shaped bacterium, *Yersinia pestis*, caused the deaths of 25 million people in fourteenth-century Europe. *Yersinia* – named after French scientist Alexandre Yersin, who identified it over 100 years ago – causes bubonic plague, the killer disease transmitted by fleas living in the fur of rats.

Bubonic Plague still rears its ugly head from time to time – both America and India have suffered from recent outbreaks. But now antibiotics can see *Yersinia* off, and it's viral diseases such as influenza and AIDS that cause the most worry. The Great Influenza Pandemic of 1918 killed an estimated 20 million people – more than twice the numbers killed fighting the World War that ended the same year.

what was the great gold crisis?

In 1925, Britain's new Chancellor of the Exchequer, Winston Churchill, announced that he was putting Britain back on the Gold Standard. First introduced by Britain in 1821, the Gold Standard was supposed to be a way of fixing exchange rates between countries. By defining currencies in terms of so much gold, each country knew where it stood: a dollar always bought a certain quantity of gold, while a pound always bought another quantity – thus the value of a dollar relative to the pound remained stable.

But while many cheered Churchill's decision, some did not. The great economist John Maynard Keynes warned that the world had been changed forever by the Great War, and that Britain was no longer the huge economic force it had been. Its dominance had been overtaken by the US, so going back to the Gold Standard risked shackling the City to the vagaries of Wall Street. Keynes' fears were quickly vindicated. Simply getting back on to the Gold Standard caused problems: it demanded the re-establishment of the pre-war dollar-pound exchange rate – which was 10 per cent higher than it had become in 1925. The sudden jump in the value of the pound badly affected UK exports and the balance of trade.

However, not even Keynes foresaw quite how bad things would become. The impact on Britain's economy precipitated the General Strike of 1926, while the effects of the Wall Street Crash of 1929 spread across the Atlantic and caused a run on Central European Banks, and pressure on the Bank of England itself. In September 1931, the British Government was forced to accept that Keynes had been right – and abandoned the Gold Standard forever.

could the population of china really all stand on the isle of wight?

Yes they could – with a bit of a squeeze. The Isle of Wight has an area of 147 square miles, which means that each of China's 1,300 million people would have a standing area of just 21 x 21 inches. Not much room for the fatties – but the tots could fit in the spaces in between.

what's the trick for working out what the day of the week will be for any given date?

For any date in the last century – say 9 February 1999 – take the final two digits of the year (99, in this case), divide that number by four (ignoring any remainder) and add the result (24) to the original digits, (99 + 24 = 123). Now add the day of the month (nine) and divide the result by seven, this time keeping only the remainder, (in this case, six). Then add the "month number". For January, the month number is six (five in leap years); February is two (one in a leap year); March is two; April five; May zero; June three; July five; August one; September four; October six; November two and December four. So, adding two for February to the six we had as our remainder gives eight. Finally, add two and divide by seven, again keeping only the remainder. In this instance, the remainder is three; the answer is the third day of the week – a Tuesday.

The same trick works for the current century – just add one instead of two before the final division by seven.

🔵 What is a bell curve?

🔵 A bell curve is literally a bell-shaped curve that appears on graphs for an amazing range of things, from the IQ of college students to the height of giraffes. First recognised by the French mathematician Abraham de Moivre around 1733, it was put to great use by the German mathematician Carl Gauss; as a result, it is now often known by many scientists as the Gaussian curve. Put simply, the curve reflects the fact that measurements of, say, the heights of many people will produce an average figure, with relatively few having heights above or below this average.

At first glance, any curve with a peak in the middle and sloping sides would seem to show this – even a triangle. But Gauss proved that, if the spread in heights is caused by random factors, then the curve will have a very specific shape – the famous bell shape that fits measurements of many natural phenomena – so many, in fact, that scientists once thought that it explained all of them.

While this is now known to be false – for example, the frequency of lottery ball number appearances is not a bell curve – it does work for a huge range of phenomena, whose relevant curves can be described by just two numbers: the mean value, which fixes the peak of the bell curve, and the so-called standard deviation, which shows how the curve spreads out to either side of that average. Putting these two numbers into Gauss's formula then gives the percentages of, say, men whose heights are so many centimetres above or below the average. For example, a recent Department of Health survey showed that the heights of young men in Britain follows a bell curve, with an average height at 176.6cm (5ft 9$^{1/2}$in), and a standard deviation of 6.95 cm (2$^{7/10}$in). Gauss's formula shows that this implies, for example, that only 5 per cent of young men are above 188cm (6ft 2in) tall.

How do we know the size of the world's population?

No one claims to know the exact number of people alive. Experts estimate global population by adding up the census returns from each country in the world. As some of the figures can't be trusted, they make adjustments based on birth and death rates and emigration to arrive at a reliable total.

Figures can vary between organisations. The United Nations estimated that the world population reached six billion on 12 October 1999, but the US Census Department put the date at 19 June 1999. A world population of six billion means an estimated increase of 145 per cent in the last 50 years, but this is no reliable guide to future growth.

For what it's worth – which may not be very much – a recent report from the UN's Population Division states that the world's population will increase from 6.1 billion to 9.3 billion during the next 50 years. This sounds frightening, until one recalls that back in 1984, the talk was of the world's population heading towards 12 billion people by the end of the 21st century. The UN World Population Conference said then that Mexico City had become the world's most populous city, packed with 17 million people, and predicted that it would swell to 26 million people by the year 2000.

But in 1996, a comprehensive re-analysis of the whole population issue showed that the world's population looks set to peak at less than 11 billion around 2080, and then fall back again. As for Mexico City, the experts now admit that its population never even reached 17 million in the first place and is never likely to make 26 million at all.

Has a tossed coin ever landed on its edge?

Yes, it has, and in front of dozens of witnesses. On 9 October 1972, the mathematician Dr Jeff Hamilton was giving a lecture on probability theory at Warwick University and wanted to show his students the effect of chance by tossing a coin. He took a 2p coin out of his pocket and tossed it high in the air. When it landed it spun round rapidly, before slowly coming to rest – on its edge. According to Dr Hamilton, around 40 students witnessed the amazing event and, after a stunned silence they broke into wild applause. Statisticians reckon that the chances of it happening were around one in a billion.

Do other animals outnumber humans?

Yes, easily. There are twice as many chickens (around 12 billion) as people in the world, and more cattle on the planet than there are people in China (1.3 billion). And while it's true that there's only one sheep per 5.62 people on average, they're not evenly spread over the globe – so in the Falkland Islands, for example, they outnumber humans by a whopping 338 to one.

The uneven distribution of animals means that Brazil, Argentina, Australia and Ireland all have more cattle than people, Somalia has twice as many goats as humans and top of the pig league is Denmark: 9.5 million porkers against 5.2 million humans. No country has more camels than humans, though Somalia, with nearly seven million, tops the camel chart way ahead of anywhere else. Oddly, Egypt – which seems to base its entire tourism industry around camel trips to the pyramids – comes in a lowly sixteenth in the camel league, with a mere 200,000.

How many colours would it take to guarantee that no country on a map is the same colour as its neighbour?

Take a sheet of paper and draw your own map on it, made up of lots of countries sharing borders. Now colour in the map. You'll find that no matter how complicated you make it, you'll never need more than four different colours to ensure no two neighbouring countries share the same colour. Since this odd fact was first pointed out in 1851, many mathematicians tried to find the reason for what became known as the notorious "four colour theorem"; some even thought they had solved it – only to be proved wrong years later.

It took almost 40 years just to prove that no more than five colours were needed. Going the final step to four colours took over a century, and was achieved in 1976 by two mathematicians, Wolfgang Haken and Kenneth Appel, at the University of Illinois, assisted by a supercomputer. Essentially, they boiled the problem down until they were left with just 1,936 arrangements of borders that could turn up in any map. They then set their supercomputer to work, proving that every one of these arrangements still led to maps needing no more than four colours. The final proof took over 1,000 hours of supercomputer time – and takes up hundreds of pages.

🔢 is the mastermind game like real code-breaking?

🔢 Mastermind has been a bestseller ever since it first hit the toyshops in 1973. The aim of the game is to work out the secret "code" of four coloured pegs chosen by an opponent. Random guessing isn't advised: there are eight varieties of peg from which the four are selected, making 4,096 possible codes from which to choose – but you get only 12 attempts to succeed. So the smart approach is to exploit clues about how accurate each attempt has been. Good players find that the more attempts they make, the harder it becomes to find arrangements of pegs consistent with all the previous clues. If a set of pegs produces no contradictions it is invariably the correct code.

The astonishing power of contradictions to weed out bad answers and focus in on the right ones was exploited by code breakers tackling the Nazi Enigma cipher. Although the Enigma machine generated more than 10 million billion combinations, the Allied code breakers were often able to read messages, using the Mastermind method of clues-plus-contradictions. For example, the design of the Enigma machine meant that it was impossible for a letter to be encoded into itself – that is, an "E" could never be encoded as an "E". On the other hand, if "E" was encoded into, say, "Y", then it was also true that "Y" would be turned into an "E". These subtle design flaws were exploited by code-breakers at Bletchley Park, who used machines to crank through the various possible settings of Enigma machines – and throw out ones that led to contradictions, such as letters being encoded as themselves.

🅐 why are the queues for women's toilets always so long?

🅑 Women simply take longer – around 2.3 times longer, according to an international study (don't ask) by Professor Alexander Kira of Cornell University. But this doesn't mean that the queues are just 2.3 times longer. In 2000, one of the *Focus* magazine editors used a branch of mathematics called – amazingly enough – queuing theory to prove a mathematical rule which he calls the Law of Inconvenience: if a queue moves X times more slowly than another, then that queue will be at least X-squared times longer, and people in it will also typically have to wait X-squared times longer. So that means that women can typically expect to queue at least 2.3-squared – i.e. five times – longer for the toilet than men.

So what's the answer to this long-standing problem? Simple: women should be given at least 2.3 times as many toilets. The same Law of Inconvenience explains why some supermarket queues are longer than others: if a checkout person is X times slower than average – say, because he's a trainee – his queue will be X-squared times longer. So, for example, if the spotty trainee is just 25 per cent slower than the veterans on the tills, his queue will be over 50 per cent longer.

Is it true that the checkout queue you're in is usually beaten by the one next to you?

If you join a queue behind a family of 10 shopping for the winter, then of course you get what you deserve. Yet, even if all the queues are essentially the same length, and being served at the same average rate, it's still true that the queue you're in will usually get beaten by the one next to you. The reason is pretty simple: when you go to a supermarket checkout, there are just three queues you care about: the one you chose, plus the two to either side, by which you can see how good a choice you've made. All three are equally prone to the vagaries of people fumbling for change, the barcode reader failing and so on. But on any one visit to the supermarket, the chances you've picked the one of the three least likely to be subject to these delays, and thus finish first, is just one in three. Two times out of three – that's almost 70 per cent of the time – random factors will ensure that one of your two neighbouring queues will beat you.

It's just like throwing dice: on average, any number is as likely to come up as any other, but the chances of your number coming up on a specific occasion is just 1 in 6. Can you do anything about it? Well, not really – though you could try going to the checkouts nearest the walls. That way, you'll only have one neighbour to compare your progress with, and thus boost your chances of finishing first from just 33 per cent to 50 per cent.

Why does the financial year start in April?

The bizarre timing of the financial year is a hang-over from the days when the New Year was taken to begin on 25 March – the Feast of the Annunciation, exactly nine months before Christ's birthday. That all changed in 1752, when Britain adopted the Gregorian calendar, a reform which switched New Year's day to 1 January, but left the financial year unchanged. The reform also added 10 days on to the old calendar dates, so that the start of the financial year was shunted from the last week of March to the first week of April – and it's stayed there ever since.

How big an area of land could be destroyed if every nuclear bomb went off?

Not as big as you might think. There are about 15,000 nuclear warheads in the world, with a combined explosive power equivalent to around 10,000 megatons (MT) of TNT. Just one British Trident submarine has 10 times the destructive capability of all the bombs dropped in World War II.

But studies of the effect of explosives – both conventional and nuclear – have led to a rule of thumb that shows that the area, in square kilometres, devastated by an explosion is equal to the megatonnage raised to the two-thirds power, times 200. So a 10-MT hydrogen bomb can devastate around 1,000 sq km of land. By that reckoning, 10,000 MT should clear out an area of around 1,000,000 sq km – which is less than ten times the area of England.

The fact is that to actually change the world's topography requires the enormous power of natural forces such as volcanoes, which can erupt with far more violence than anything humans can create. When the volcanic island of Krakatoa in Indonesia self-destructed in 1883, the sound of the eruption could be heard 3,000 miles away in Madagascar. More violent still are meteor impacts; the one that pushed the dinosaurs into extinction 65 million years ago is estimated to have delivered the explosive power of 10 million H-bombs.

Why are there so many odd socks in drawers?

Because of Murphy's Law of Odds Socks: "If socks can go missing, they will do" – a result that *Focus* magazine first revealed to an appalled world in 1996. To see why there really is a law of odd socks, imagine a drawer containing nothing but complete pairs of socks with not an odd sock in sight. Now, suppose one sock goes missing at random (don't worry about which one, or where, or how – it's irrelevant). Its loss will automatically leave an odd sock behind in the drawer. The rot has now set in. When another sock goes missing, it could be either that one odd sock now in the drawer, or it could be a sock from one of the many as-yet unbroken pairs still remaining. Clearly, it's far more likely to be the latter – thus creating yet another odd sock. And so the process continues.

Take it further with combinatorics – the mathematics of arrangements – and the results are truly frightening. For instance, suppose you start with a drawer of 10 complete pairs, and you lose just six socks at random. It's then 100 times more likely that you'll be left with the worst possible outcome – six odd socks – than with a drawer free of the things. In general, losing just half of the socks in your drawer will cut the number of complete pairs by three-quarters – and leave them lost in a sea of odd socks. Small wonder that a pair is so hard to find in the morning.

Murphy's Law of Odd Socks makes finding matching pairs a chore even after you've weeded out all the odd socks. If you have 10 complete pairs of socks mixed up in your drawer, you'll typically have to rummage through about 30 per cent of them before finding just one matching pair.

What can you do? You could, of course, go to great lengths to ensure socks don't go astray in the wash, by pinning them together or putting them in pillowcases. The Sad Person's solution is to ditch all their different socks, and replace them with identical ones. The mathematics of odd socks offers a slightly less draconian solution: choose two sock varieties, and stick to them. Socks of each type will then go missing at more or less the same rate, and whatever complete pairs do remain won't be lost among zillions of odd socks. Better still, a moment's thought shows you're guaranteed to get a matching pair after drawing out just three socks.

what is the mathematical relationship between population growth and food production?

In 1798, the English economist Thomas Malthus famously argued that the human race was doomed to starve, as populations grow exponentially – that is, like 2, 4, 8, 16, 32 etc – while resources like food grows only arithmetically, like 2, 4, 6, 8, 10 and so on. What he reckoned without were the miracles of agriculture, which have radically boosted fertility of soil, killed off pests and increased crop yields.

Some of the biggest breakthroughs have come from using biotechnology to allow crops to grow in places they formerly couldn't. Recently, American plant scientists announced the discovery of a gene that will allow wheat to grow in acidic soil. Acidic soil is often relatively rich in aluminium, which normally stunts crop growth. The discovery is likely to make wheat production possible on an extra 5,000 million acres of land. Chinese scientists have also claimed to have found a way of boosting the output of rice plants by using seedlings that have been reared in space. The scientists think that a combination of low gravity and radiation plays a role in altering the gene structure of the plants.

Scientists are also hoping to get crops to grow in drought regions using a natural water-saving process called Crassulacean Acid Metabolism (CAM), which allows plants to take advantage of cooler night temperatures to minimise water loss. Scientists at the University of Nevada have recently identified hundreds of genes that they think are associated with drought resistance. By inserting the right genes into crops, they hope to be able to increase food production in countries susceptible to drought. Even without all of these advances the fact is that the world already produces more food than it can eat. The problem is that too much is produced in some places and not enough in others. A fairer system of distribution could, in theory, put an end to all famine today.

Q: what's the weirdest form of currency?

A: Primitive cultures tended to improvise their promissory tokens before money became formalised. Common examples of currency among them included specially shaped stones, cowrie shells, cattle, manillas (a type of jewellery) and, in Fiji, whales' teeth, which were used as "bride-money". Similar tokens were still in use in North America as recently as the 1960s.

One of the benefits of using cattle as a currency is that they can, like coins, be counted, though many African tribes would take into account neither age nor weight of the cows, which made the value system very difficult to sustain. Until well into this century the Kirghiz people of the Russian steppes used horses as their main currency, with sheep as a subsidiary unit.

Q: is it true that you're more likely to be hit by a bus while on the way to buy a lottery ticket than you are to hit the jackpot?

A: According to the Department of Transport, buses and coaches hit 37 people for every 100 million vehicle kilometres driven. So let's assume that buying your Lottery ticket involves you making a journey of around 1km along a perilously bus-infested road. Assuming that everyone is at equal risk from stray No. 18s, that means that you've got about a 1 in 3 million chance of being flattened during your foray to get your Lottery ticket. Your chances of winning, on the other hand, are four times worse, at a dismally low 1 in 14 million. So don't risk it – stay at home instead.

Q: what is the furthest that a car can travel on one gallon of petrol?

A: A unique French car called the Microjoule can do an amazing 9,845 miles on just one gallon of petrol. It was one of 120 cars to take part in the 1999 Shell Eco-Marathon, in which young people from all over the world had to develop a vehicle to travel as many miles as possible on a single gallon of fuel. The Microjoule cost £13,000 and 10,000 man hours to build. The trouble is, there is only one of them. If it's a commercial green machine you want, Volkswagen has launched the three-litre Lupo TDI which, it says, can do 94 mpg, a world-best for a production road vehicle.

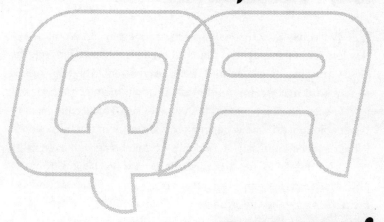

good
good
question
question

can you see the Apollo moon landing sites using the Hubble space Telescope?

For conspiracy theorists seeking proof that NASA made the whole Apollo thing up and filmed it on a Hollywood film set, the HST's amazing powers would seem heaven-sent. The telescope is so powerful that it can pick out details down to an angular size of just 0.1 seconds of arc – 1/36,000th of a degree. That's equivalent to being able to read a newspaper from a distance of two kilometres. Which is very impressive – the only trouble being that even at its closest to the Earth, the Moon is still around 363,000km from the HST. That prevents it making out anything smaller than around 180 metres across – and unfortunately the Lunar Module which NASA used (allegedly) to put astronauts on the Moon was barely 10 metres across.

why are motorways lit with orange lights?

The main reason is that the so-called high-pressure sodium lights that light up motorways are very efficient – that is, they produce a lot of light for a given amount of electricity, making them ideal as a cost-effective means of lighting up Britain's major roads. However, it's not all economics – there are a couple of good scientific reasons, too. The first is that at night-time the human eye is most sensitive to orange light – which is exactly what high-pressure sodium lights put out. Secondly, the longer the wavelength of light, the less likely it is to get scattered by the water droplets in fog and mist. So if you're looking for a lamp that will send its beams deep into the gloom of a November night, *and* give drivers illumination best suited to their eyes, high-pressure sodium lights are pretty much ideal.

On the occasions that you do see white lights on the motorway, they are normally illuminating round-the-clock construction work.

Are all those "ordinary punters" in TV ads really professional actors?

We've all seen those adverts: people apparently straight off the street giving their totally unbiased opinion of a soap-powder or soup. But everyone knows they're not ordinary people – all of them are paid-up actors, right? Well, no, actually. It's a myth that Equity, (the actors' trade union), operates a "closed shop" with TV, preventing anyone but union members from appearing on-screen. Such restrictions have been illegal in Britain since union-busting legislation was introduced by Margaret Thatcher in 1988. But even before then, ordinary people could and did appear in TV adverts. It seems that some people really do like those soap-powders and soups after all.

Why are some people "double-jointed"?

It is certainly not because they have two joints in places where the rest of us have only one. The real cause of hypermobility – as the syndrome is known medically – is ligaments that are much more elastic than normal, allowing joints to reach angles that in most people wouldn't be possible.

Everyone can attain some level of hypermobility through exercise – especially yoga – and many children have some hypermobile joints because their ligaments have yet to grow strong enough to restrict movement.

Those born with the syndrome can perform all sorts of amazing feats, such as bending their thumbs back to touch their forearm, sticking their little fingers out by more than 90 degrees, and bending their knees left and right, as well as forward.

It's a trait that tends to run in families, especially in those with tall fathers. Those with hypermobility often become excellent gymnasts and dancers. But there is a dark side to the condition as well – patients often suffer more than their fair share of injuries, aches and pains, and run a higher risk of developing osteoarthritis.

Q: was the orange named after its colour or was the colour named after the fruit?

A: According to the experts at the *Oxford English Dictionary*, the fruit came first. The origin of the word orange used to describe the fruit dates back thousands of years to the Sanskrit word "naranga". The earliest reference to eatable oranges in English appears in a manuscript written in 1387. On the other hand, the first use of the word orange to describe a colour appears in a collection of poems by the Scots poet Alexander Montgomerie, published much later, in 1600.

Q: what's the sharpest object ever made?

A: Even the sharpest needle looks blunt compared to a bee sting. You'd hardly feel it going into the skin at all, were it not for the pain-inducing poison that the bee squirts in with it. The accolade for the sharpest object goes not to the bee sting, however, but to the tip of a scanning tunnelling microscope (STM). Invented in 1980 by scientists at IBM, the STM uses an electric current flowing between its tip and the surface of a target object to map the contours of that object's individual atoms. To pull off this feat the tip is just 0.1 millionths of a millimetre across – the width of a few atoms. Now that's sharp.

Q: why do wagon-wheels sometimes seem to go backwards in movies?

A: It's a symptom of the fact that movies are made up of individual frames shot at the rate of 24 per second. If a wagon-wheel is also turning at the rate of 24 spokes a second, the position of a spoke in one frame will have been taken up by another spoke in the next frame – thus giving the appearance that nothing has changed, and that the wheel isn't moving at all. But if the wheel is moving slightly slower than 24 spokes a second, each spoke does not quite have enough time to get into position by the time the next movie frame is taken, and instead appears slightly behind the spoke that appeared in the previous frame. The result is a wagon-wheel that appears to be running backwards.

why was mozart so impoverished?

With his combination of genius and sheer hard work, one might think that Mozart would have made a fortune out of his music. After all, Andrew Lloyd Webber has amassed a personal fortune of over £350 million from his work. Unluckily for Mozart, however, he lived at the end of the eighteenth century. Not only was there no recording industry, but there were no laws of copyright either. As a result, Mozart did not make a penny from repeat performances of his symphonies, or from sales of his sheet music. In contrast, Lloyd Webber makes money every time his music is performed.

While Mozart was never rich, and was reduced to asking for loans towards the end of his life, he was never as poor as some have claimed. During his best years as a freelance musician in Vienna, he and his wife lived in a smart high-rent apartment, and they never had to do without a servant. The problem – as for most freelancers – was his irregular income, which he tried to smooth out with teaching.

Mozart's resentment of authority didn't help either. He refused to suck up to aristocrats who might offer commissions or positions at court, and his antics annoyed those who did give him work. His attitude was always that his sheer talent would see him through: "Our riches, being in our brains, die with us – and these no man can take from us unless he chops off our heads," he told his father. Mozart was certainly right about his riches being in his brains. Unfortunately for him, he was born too soon for his riches to be in his pockets as well.

why does the red paint on road signs fade so much?

It's not just the red paint on road-signs: check out anything decorated in bright colours – cars, clothes, toys – and you'll see that the red parts have faded most of all. The reason lies in the fact that daylight is made from a rainbow-like spectrum, and red objects bounce back the red component of daylight into our eyes – which is why we see them as red in the first place. On the other hand, they absorb all the other colours, which all have shorter wavelengths. These shorter-wavelength colours have relatively high energies – high enough to break apart the molecules making up red pigments. As a result, red fades away much more rapidly than any other colour.

could a grandmaster memorise all the possible moves in chess?

Only if they had a brain the size of the universe. Each position in chess opens up around 38 legally valid moves – which means that the number of possible arrangements of chess pieces grows with awesome speed the further you get in into the game. For example, after each player has made just three moves, the number of possibilities opened up has ballooned to 38^6, or 3 billion. And with chess games routinely going to over 40 moves by each player, the total number of possible positions is at least 10^{126}. To give some idea of how big this number is, there have only been 10^{17} seconds since the Big Bang, and there are merely 10^{80} sub-atomic particles in the entire cosmos.

So why do grandmasters bother to study previous games, when they represent just a tiny drop in the vast ocean of possible moves? They do it because chess is not simply a matter of making legal but random moves; the moves in real games have winning strategy and tactics driving them – making the positions they create well worth remembering.

Q: what is the temperature of space?

A: It depends where – and when – you're talking about. At the distance the Earth is from the Sun, the sun's heat warms space to around 123℃ (not that we get much of that, because the Earth's atmosphere and surface bounces most of it back). But go out into the very depths of space, far from any galaxy, and the temperature drops to a desperately low -270℃, just three degrees above Absolute Zero, the coldest temperature theoretically possible. And the cosmos is set to get even colder. Those 3 degrees are all that's left of the colossal heat of the Big Bang around 12 billion years ago; as time rolls on, the temperature will drop lower still.

Q: why is lead crystal so-called?

A: Despite its glamorous image, lead crystal is just a form of glass. First made in the 1670s by the glass-maker George Ravenscroft, this so-called flint glass turned out to have very impressive optical properties, including a great sparkle. Early samples suffered from surface cracks – a problem solved by adding an oxide of lead to the mix. The result was a form of glass with far more sparkle than ordinary glass and even more colourful "fire" than diamond. Lead crystal soon became popular in the form of spectacular chandeliers, jewellery, ornaments and glassware.

Nowadays, we know that lead crystal is best looked at but not used. Research has shown that the lead oxide can leach out of decanters and glasses leading to potentially harmful levels of lead in the wines and spirits they contain.

Q: why are magic mushrooms magic?

A: One of the best-known kinds of magic mushroom – the Fly Agaric – is easy to spot. It's that red and white toadstool that fairies like to sit on. But be warned: in Britain, magic mushrooms are classed as an illegal substance, even though they're available in the wild – and messing with them can be lethal.

Those who use magic mushrooms often report vivid visual illusions in which objects seem smaller or larger than they actually are. Lewis Carroll used magic mushrooms and they may have offered the inspiration for the often larger-than-life adventures Alice underwent in Wonderland.

Siberians swear by Fly Agaric to give them the stamina to fling off their snowshoes and stride barefoot through the snow. In order to get the most out of their fungi, they wash them down with a glassful of their own urine.

How smart are plants?

Okay, you won't get a yucca on University Challenge any time soon, but plants are far more sophisticated than you might think. "During the process of germination even tiny seeds can sense 20 different factors, such as the time of year and positioning of light, which they use to determine the right time to germinate," says Professor Anthony Trewavas of Edinburgh University.

Plants also have feelings – in the sense of being able to detect the presence of other organisms. The most famous meat-eating plant, the Venus flytrap, has evolved a sense of touch, so that when an insect brushes against its trigger hairs, the plant's "jaws" close and trap the hapless creature inside.

Darwin was among the first to suggest this action mimics the response of a human nervous system. To see if there was any truth in Darwin's suggestion, John Burdon-Sanderson, a medical physiologist at University College London, strapped electrodes to a flytrap. He discovered that when a trigger hair is touched, it generates an electrical impulse similar to a human nerve impulse. The speed of response, however, is very different. In a human, the impulse travels at 100 metres a second, while in the plant it's thousands of times more sluggish, at just three centimetres a second.

Perhaps the most impressive example of a "quick" plant reaction can be seen in the *Mimosa pudica*. Found in the rainforests of Borneo, it is known as the "sensitive" plant. If you touch its leaves, they will fold up within seconds. The cause of the movement in the sensitive plant is a rapid influx of calcium into its cells.

More than 1,000 species of plant, in 17 different families, are touch-sensitive. They almost certainly inherited this response from cyanobacteria, the ancestors of all plant life, which can react to stimuli by producing tiny electrical signals.

what's the logic behind London's postal districts?

Having the right postcode in London can do wonders for the price of your house, but the coding system in use today seems to have little geographical logic. There is, however, a reason for it.

In the first half of the nineteenth century, before any postal divisions existed, a letter addressed to 10 George Street, London could have been intended for any one of 62 George Streets in the London area. The resulting confusion led Dr Rowland Hill to devise the first postcode system in 1857. He divided London into districts: SE, W, WC (C for Central), EC, E, SW, N, NW and NE. (There were no NE or S districts – these were assimilated into E and SE/SW.) So far, so clear.

The trouble started when these ten districts were subdivided by number – for example, W1 or EC3 – in 1916. The move was prompted by the fact that many post office sorters were away fighting in World War I. So, to ensure the inexperienced sorters wouldn't make a complete mess of things, the districts were subdivided in alphabetical order. For example, Bethnal Green became E2 and Bow became E3. Geographical proximity to the centre counted for nothing.

good question

The system was tweaked slightly between 1968 and 1971 as part of a nationwide recording programme. For London this meant the creation of additional internal codes for the crowded districts of SE and SW (such as SW1E). It may look confusing, but it seems to have worked well for the sorters.

what is the oldest living thing on earth?

Pinus longaeva – better known as the bristlecone pine of Nevada. The oldest one is almost 4,800 years old.

While scientists have long known of trees whose growth-rings revealed ages of many centuries, no one suspected just how old these wizened mountain pines were until the 1950s. Curiously, the oldest trees were found in the driest, least hospitable regions, with several being more than 3,000 years old. The oldest of all, identified in 1957, proved to have first sprouted back in 2766 BC. The aptly-named Methuselah is still going strong today, aged 4,767. To give some idea of how old Methuselah the pine tree is, it was already 66 years old when the pharaoh Khufu ordered the construction of the Great Pyramid of Giza, and was middle-aged when Athens made peace with Sparta.

is it true that, if you fall from a tall building, you die before hitting the ground?

It's a widely held belief that if you were to fall from the top of a high building you would die of shock before hitting the ground. But it's a myth. While it is possible that the shock of falling could trigger a fatal cardiac arrest, the chances are that your demise will be the result of hitting the ground. That said, people have survived falls from tremendous heights – it all depends upon how and where you land. If you end up in a snowdrift where the impact is cushioned, you are far more likely to survive than if you land on a pavement.

In January 1942, Lt I M Chisov fell 6,700m (almost 22,000ft) from his wrecked Ilyushin 4 aircraft without a parachute and survived – he struck the edge of a snow-covered gully and slid to an eventual halt. Air hostess Vesna Vulovic topped that in 1972 when by descending over 10,000 metres (33,300ft) without a parachute when the DC9 she was in disintegrated over Czechoslovakia – she was in the tail-section of the plane.

Once you fall out of anything above around 2000ft (600m) up in the air, it makes little difference how high up you were. Air resistance means that you'll have reached the aptly-named terminal velocity of around 120mph after falling this distance – and you won't go any faster, no matter what height you started from – it just takes longer for you to hit the deck!

📷 is there any truth to claims of people developing foreign accents after bangs on the head?

📷 Strangely, yes – it's a rare but well-documented phenomenon. There are about 50 cases of Foreign Accent Syndrome listed in the medical literature. It arises when various connections to the speech control centre in the left side of the brain are damaged and a different language pattern emerges.

A recent victim was Steward Rayner from East London. He fractured his skull in an autosport accident in 1997 and when he regained consciousness, his usual cockney accent had transformed into a southern US drawl. In the same year, an English woman who had suffered a cerebral haemorrhage found herself speaking French with a perfect accent.

A particularly sad case occurred durng the Second World War, when a Norwegian woman was hit on the head by shrapnel during a German air raid. She fell into a deep coma and woke up with a German accent.

How do seedless grapes reproduce?

Technically, they don't. You just have to keep taking and replanting cuttings from the leaf or stem of the plants. Seedless grapes – grown in Chile, Greece, India and North America – have been bred selectively over the years for people who hate spitting out the pips. Some actually do have small seeds, which people unknowingly swallow, but they are only partially formed and could not grow into plants if left in the wild. This commercial agricultural technique – called vegetative propagation – is also used to grow seedless bananas.

Do women and children still get to enter lifeboats first?

This particular aspect of maritime gallantry has never been enshrined in any set of regulations, directives or codes of seagoing practice. It's just a case of decent chaps electing to do the right thing. Extremely decent, in fact, because it frequently cost them their lives: when the *Titanic* was struck by an iceberg on 14 April 1912, there were lifeboats for barely half the 2,200 on board – and men routinely gave up their chances to save the lives of the women and children.

The need to make such decisions became less common after 1914, when the International Maritime Organization (IMO) convened a meeting to introduce new laws for passenger safety. The result was the Safety Of Life At Sea convention, which, although it has often been amended, still applies today. It compels ship owners to provide enough lifeboats to evacuate all of their passengers.

According to spokesmen from P&O Stena Ferries, the "women and children first" sentiment would still prevail even on Channel crossings. Under the sea, however, tradition counts for little – the Channel Tunnel rail company Eurostar says that in the event of an evacuation, the only people who would get priority would be the disabled.

🙋 what does the "mi" in mi5 and mi6 stand for – and were there any others?

🗨️ The MI stands for "military intelligence", with the numbers referring to different sections. MI5 was set up in 1909 to keep an eye on German spies in Britain, and has focused on internal security ever since. MI6, formed in 1912, is officially known as the Secret Intelligence Service (SIS), and focuses on gathering and analysing intelligence. Several more sections once existed. MI1 was involved in deciphering enemy messages, MI8 focused on intercepting cable traffic, while MI9 interrogated prisoners of war. There were even sub-sections of the various sections: MI8(a) dealt with intercepting wireless traffic, MI8(b) worked on commercial and trade cables, while MI8(c) handled censorship. But they've all now been disbanded or swallowed up by MI5 or MI6.

🙋 what is the world's rarest plant?

🗨️ Until its discovery in 1994, the wollemi pine was thought to be long extinct. It was known only from fossil remains, dating back to the age of the dinosaurs, up to 200 million years ago.

Then national parks field officer David Noble came upon 38 wollemi pines, some 40 metres tall and over a thousand years old at the bottom of a 150-metre gorge in the Blue Mountains of New South Wales. Because of the importance of the discovery, the New South Wales authorities have kept the precise location a secret and have introduced draconian penalties (a £100,000 fine and a jail term) for anyone trespassing in the restricted area.

However, they have also begun a breeding and research programme for the wollemi pine – because the 38 known plants are genetically identical, and could all be wiped out by a single virus or other disease. The breeding programme should be complete by 2005, by which time the future survival of the wollemi pine should be assured.

good question

You can get left-handed guitars, so why not left-handed pianos?

There's certainly a demand for them; as most piano music has the more intricate melody in the right hand, with the left-hand playing supporting chords – and many left-handers would be more adept at playing the opposite way. Concert pianist Christopher Seed actually commissioned the first left-handed piano and debuted it at the Queen Elizabeth Hall in February, 1999. Costing £28,000, it's a mirror image of a normal piano, with the keys and pedals reversed. Seed has also developed a module for electronic keyboards, which switches the function of the right-hand and left-hand keys.

Has anyone developed grass that can mow itself?

Grass that doesn't need mowing and dwarf versions of any plant you choose may be coming to a garden near you, thanks to the discovery of the BAS-1 gene by researchers at the Salk Institute in San Diego, California.

The gene works by breaking down brassinolide, a growth hormone found in the stems of plants. If BAS-1 is switched on, the plant's growth is stunted. Because the gene is localised in the stem, the dwarfed plant looks otherwise normal.

The Salk team have used BAS-1 to stunt the growth of a tobacco plant from 6ft to just 12 inches, an effect also achieved in *Arabidopsis*, a member of the mustard family. Work continues on the possibility of stunting grass plants. Team leader Dr Joanne Chory says that geneticists will probably find genes in the future which will allow them to alter plants entirely. Fancy an orange lawn anyone?

why does the place you want so often lie on an awkward bit of the road atlas?

Because that "awkward bit" – namely, the area around the edge and down the central crease – is much bigger than it looks. Imagine a strip with a width just 10 per cent of the total width of an atlas page running around the edge of the page and down each side of the central crease. For a square map, a bit of simple geometry shows that this strip accounts for an impressive 50 per cent of the total area of the map. Although the width of the strip is relatively narrow, it follows the longest lines on the map page. As a result, its total area is much larger than you'd think – as are your chances of landing in it.

did dinosaurs really feed on treetops, as in Jurassic Park?

It made for some charming scenes in Spielberg's blockbuster film, but according to Dr Roger Seymour, of the University of Adelaide's Department of Environmental Biology, it's a biological impossibility. He says that the group of dinosaurs collectively known as sauropods could realistically only have functioned by keeping their necks horizontal. His claim is based on research into the factors that determine heart size in animals. He has spent the last 24 years collecting data on arterial blood pressure and the structure of the heart in reptiles, birds and mammals to determine how blood pressure influences the thickness of the heart wall.

His findings show that heart size in all animals depends on two factors; the vertical distance of the head above the heart, and whether the animal is cold- or warm-blooded. For example, the giraffe has exceptionally high blood pressure and an enlarged heart because it has to pump blood up its long neck. "We have determined that the muscle of the left ventricle in a warm-blooded Barosaurus, say, would have needed to weigh about 2,000kg to pump the blood its brain needed," explains Seymour. "This is impossible for at least three reasons. First, it would be difficult to fit such a heart into the available space; second, the heart would use more energy than the entire remainder of the body and third, its thick walls would be mechanically so inefficient that they'd expend more energy contracting than actually pumping up the blood."

It is just possible, he concedes, that sauropods could have had a vertical neck, with blood supplied from a smaller heart – but only if they had a low metabolic rate, typical of a cold-blooded reptile. This report will therefore add fuel to the ongoing debate amongst palaeontologists as to whether dinosaurs were warm- or cold-blooded creatures.

could a computer virus start world war III?

No – but it could play a key role once one got going. A virus is unlikely to start a war as it would not only have to infect military computer systems, but also take control of them and fool human users into believing that they were receiving orders to attack. Missile systems always have humans in the control loop so no computer could order a strike on its own. But viruses would almost certainly be a major weapon should World War III ever break out. "Information warfare" is the hot topic in military converations these days.

The Americans won the Gulf War partly by crippling Iraqi communication systems. Although we don't know whether this was achieved with viruses, viral infection of an enemy's computer communications will doubtless be used in the future.

One of the more paranoid rumours circulating in the defence establishment outside America has it that a lot of high-end software sold to foreign powers by the USA contains viral code which will activate in the event of war and paralyse the computer systems of anyone who tries to oppose the US.

why do the hairs on our heads keep on growing, while ones on our arms don't?

Hair is produced by follicles, tiny organs in the skin. These follicles operate on a three-stage cycle. The longest growing-period – when hair grows fastest – is known as anagen. Catagen is a shorter cycle, when growth slows down. And talogen is the rest period, when shedding is induced. Different parts of the body spend different amounts of time on each part of the cycle. The scalp spends as long as four to eight years in anagen before catagen begins, then a maximum of just four months in talogen, before anagen starts again. In contrast, the follicles on our arms and other body areas spend much less time in anagen – as little as one month. As a result, the hair there does not grow as much as the hair on our heads.

where is the safest place to stand outside in a thunderstorm?

When you're outdoors and it starts to rain, it seems to make sense to take shelter under the nearest tree. However, if a thunderstorm is brewing, this is the last place you should run for cover. Lightning targets the tallest earth-bound object in the area. An umbrella isn't much better, either – especially if you're in the middle of a field without a church spire or tree in sight.

If you're out in a really open space, such as a golf course, then the tallest point around may be your head. Finding your hair starting to stand on end is a tell-tale sign that you have been marked out for a direct hit.

The best advice during a thunderstorm is to try to get into a building or car. When this is not possible, the Meteorological Office advises that you look for a depression in the ground, such as a ditch or bunker. First check that it is free of water (which conducts electricity), then crouch in it, making yourself as small as possible.

Put your feet together to ensure your whole body is at the same electrical potential – and put your hands on your knees. With luck, if you do get hit, this will send the current through your arms and into your legs, missing your heart.

Rubber boots won't save you in the event of a direct hit – the incredibly high voltage makes their insulating value pretty minimal. But they can make a difference between life and death if the lightning strikes close by instead.

🌀 Are there any drugs that simulate death?

🔵 The voodoo phenomenon of zombies – in which people allegedly come back from the dead – is the result of victims being given a potion that includes tetrodotoxin, an extract from the puffer fish. Thousands of times more poisonous than cyanide, this neurotoxin can – if given in precisely the right dose – reduce heartbeat and breathing to levels detectable only by sophisticated electronic equipment. So, a doctor in a primitive clinic would pronounce a person under its effects dead. In fact, the person would be fully conscious, and aware of the horror of everything going on around them.

Over on the other side of the Atlantic, the West African bwiti cult uses a psychoactive shrub called iboga (sometimes spelt eboga or eboka) in their rituals to give an experience of "the beyond" so they can personally come to terms with death. Customer satisfaction is easily achieved, thanks to the massive doses provided by the cult leaders. People who want to join the cult are forced to consume the drug throughout an extremely long six-stage initiation ceremony, during which they collapse in a state of extreme intoxication. But overdosing on iboga can prove dangerous, even fatal. Many initiates of the Bwiti cult have unwittingly gone one stage too far during the initiation ceremony and actually experienced death itself.

what causes a tree to split in two, and how does it survive afterwards?

Trees tend to split as a result of decay of their so-called vascular bundles – tissue which allows water and nutrients to spread up from the roots and into the rest of the tree. The loss of large branches in storms or lightning strikes can cause massive disruption to these bundles, causing the cambium – which creates the tree's cell tissues – to die and no longer produce wood. The weakened tree may then split.

Splitting is not necessarily fatal for the tree, however. In the case of a 1,200-year-old oak at Marton in Cheshire, the split was caused by pollarding. This was a common practice 150–200 years ago; upper branches were removed to induce multiple growth for wood to use as firewood or (in the case of oaks) structural timber for boats and houses. Although the Marton oak's affected tissues are now dead, its younger, outer shell lives on. Mike Ellison, from the Ancient Tree Forum, says: "If managed properly, this tree could survive indefinitely."

where, when, how and why did snowboarding take off?

Snowboarding was conceived in 1963, when a boy named Tom Sims from New Jersey decided to design a "ski-board" as his woodwork class Christmas project. Three years later, Sherman Poppen invented the "Snurfer" – two skis stuck together. He patented his design and snow-surfing took off in the USA.

The world's first downhill Snurfer competition was on 18 February 1968 in Michigan. The race was straight downhill. Little did the racers know that exactly thirty years on, snowboarding would be featuring in the Olympics.

good question

🅠 Has anyone ever attempted to cross-breed humans with chimps?

🅐 Rumours of mad scientists trying to create "chimp-human hybrids" have been circulating for years – pretty much since it was discovered that chimps and humans have over 98 per cent of their DNA in common. But if any scientists have actually tried it, they'd certainly have to be pretty mad.

Chimps and humans still have hundreds of genes unique to themselves, and they're packaged up differently too. Humans have 46 chromosomes, while chimps have 48. Getting such different genetic constructions to work together to create a viable living creature is not possible using current techniques – and may never be.

Even so, conspiracy theorists thought they'd hit gold in 1996, when "Oliver the Human Chimp" hit the headlines. Walking upright and with curiously human gestures, Oliver had worked on the US freak show circuit since the 1970s. Lurid stories of Oliver being a hybrid eventually led to a series of genetic tests. These revealed that he was 100 per cent chimp – albeit a pretty weird one.

🅠 Can DNA help us trace the evolution of man?

🅐 Yes, it can. Because we inherit our DNA from our ancestors, it is proving extremely useful to researchers trying to unravel the history of humans.

So far, research has focused on so-called mitochondrial DNA (mtDNA) found in the energy-producing mitochondria inside each human cell. While mtDNA makes up only a tiny fraction of the total DNA in a human cell, there are hundreds of copies of mtDNA in each one. This gives researchers a much better chance of finding some intact in extremely old cell samples, such as those from fossil human bones. It is also inherited more or less intact from mother to daughter – thus giving a clearer picture of the fate of its carriers. It is already answering big questions about human origins.

In 1997, scientists successfully extracted mtDNA from the bones of Neanderthals at least 30,000 years old. Analysis of the DNA sequence proved that Neanderthals were only cousins, rather than direct ancestors, of modern humans. And last year, a study of the genetic code of people world-wide revealed that our true ancestors left Africa to spread across the world just 50,000 years ago – far more recently than previously thought.

As green plants create oxygen, how come we do not run short of it in the winter?

Oxygen forms about 21 per cent of the air we breathe (virtually all the rest being the rather inert gas, nitrogen). The seasonal difference in oxygen levels is only a few parts per million, and so is very difficult to detect. When trees shed their leaves in winter, more sunlight is able to reach ground – with the result that some plants, such as grasses, are able to photosynthesise more and make up some of the deficit. If temperatures drop, photosynthesis will slow down, but then so will respiration – the process that uses up oxygen in plants and animals. The net result is no significant changes in oxygen levels, no matter what time of the year it isks.

How does a magician saw a woman in half?

This unnerving trick was first performed 75 years ago in London by a magician who was known simply as Selbit. However, it was an American, Horace Goldin, who truly made the illusion his own. Goldin's method relied on using not one but two women. One woman was concealed in the base of Goldin's cabinet, so the audience could see only her legs protruding from

good question

the box. The other woman, whose head was exposed, had her legs pulled up to her shoulders, allowing Goldin to slice all the way through the cabinet and "through" the woman without any blood being spilt.

Other methods have used just one woman, and the "magic" has been done not with hidden assistants but fake legs or trick saws. The latter have blades that automatically become detached the instant before they make contact with the "victim" and then reconnect to another blade immediately after appearing to have passed through her.

🔵 Does getting cold and wet make you more likely to catch a cold?

🔵 Next time your mum tells you to dry your hair when you come in from the pouring rain "before you catch a cold", put on a patronising smile and tell her quietly: "Mum – colds are caused by viruses, not raindrops". It's true. While getting cold and wet might make you miserable, there is no good evidence that it increases the risk of falling prey to a cold virus.

Indeed, sharing an umbrella to keep dry is much more risky – as the person you're huddling under the umbrella with may be harbouring a cold. Or there could be cold viruses lurking on the handle. The best way to avoid colds is to avoid contact with people – or anything they've touched.

So why are colds called "colds"? The short answer is that nobody knows: according to the *Oxford English Dictionary*, the term first appeared in 1537, in the State Papers of Henry VIII. Suggestions that the King removed the heads of two of his six wives to avoid catching colds from them is not generally taken seriously by historians.

❓ What does the "D" in D-Day stand for?

🅐 There has always been speculation on why 6 June 1944 became known as D-Day. Some thought that the D stood for "Deliverance". There was also an absurd idea that it came from General Charles de Gaulle being unable to say the word "this", so pronouncing it as "D-Day" instead of "this day".

In fact, the D in D-Day is Army jargon. "M" stands for minute, "H" for hour and "D" for day. Originally, it was called simply D1, or the first day of the Allied invasion of Europe.

D-Day was a deliberately content-free term and the invasion's code name, Operation Overlord, was kept secret prior to the landings. Standard Army vocabulary has since been appropriated into general usage, so D-Day can mean any day on which a large-scale operation is due to begin.

❓ Could we grow "intelligent" plants which tell us when they need watering?

🅐 The ability to ask for water would be more than just a handy feature for plants living in bed-sits with negligent owners. Many crops give no sign of needing to be watered until they start to wilt, and by then it's often too late to save the plant.

A team of researchers from the University of Edinburgh is on the case, however. It has introduced a fluorescent gene from a jellyfish into the leaves of the potato plant, so that when the plant becomes dehydrated, it forms a protein that triggers the gene, making it glow. This can't be seen by the naked eye, but is visible using a hand-held monitor.

The research isn't expected to lead to fields of glowing spuds, however. Only a few "marker" plants would need to be added to a crop to gauge whether there was enough water. These could be removed from the crop before harvesting.

good question

❓ is it true that Bank Holidays have worse weather than ordinary mondays?

Ⓐ We've all planned barbecues or trips to the seaside for a Bank Holiday Monday only to open the curtains on the day itself to find rain pouring down. But are Bank Holidays really an example of Murphy's Law of Weather: "If it can rain on your day off, it will do?".

Meteorologist Philip Eden has studied the records – and it seems we're all suffering from a case of selective memory, where we just remember the time when our holiday plans were ruined, and forget when the sun shined on them.

Eden compared the weather on public holidays with that on adjacent weekends from 1990 to 2000. He found that the May Day and late-spring holidays both gave better weather than neighbouring weekends, while the August bank holiday weekend was neither better nor worse. Only in the case of Easter – which moves around a lot – was Murphy's Law of Weather confirmed, and then only marginally, with the weather being worse just 55 per cent of the time.

about the editors

Robert Matthews and Nick Smith were contemporaries at the University of Oxford in the early 1980s.

Robert went on to become science consultant to *Focus* magazine, and a physicist at Aston University. His best-known research is on why toast lands butter-side down, which won him an Ig Nobel prize in 1996.

Nick went on to become the longest-serving editor on *Focus*. He has won several journalism awards and is currently writing a book about Cuban cigars.

index